THE COLOUR ENCYCLOPEDIA OF
INCREDIBLE AEROPLANES

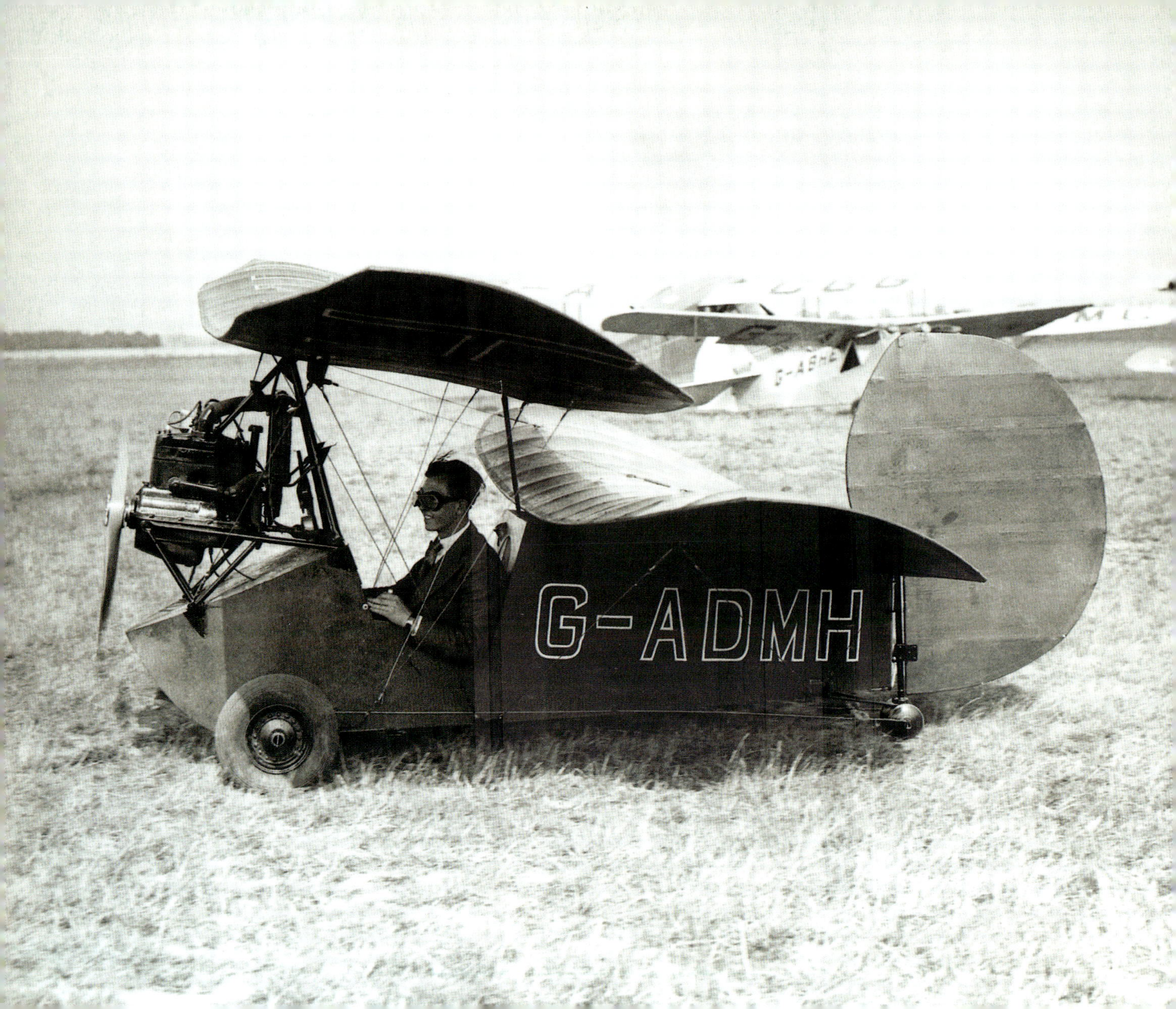
G-ADMH

THE COLOUR ENCYCLOPEDIA OF
INCREDIBLE AEROPLANES

Philip Jarrett

DK

LONDON, NEW YORK, MELBOURNE,
MUNICH, DELHI

Project Editor Amber Tokeley
Senior Art Editor Mandy Earey
Designers Clare Joyce, Peter Laws, Loan Nguyen
Editorial Consultant Reg Grant
Picture Research Kate Lockley
Illustrators Debajyoti Dutta, Mugdha Sethi
Production Editor Sarah Sherlock
Production Controller Inderjit Bhullar

Managing Editor Julie Oughton
Managing Art Editor Christine Keilty
Publisher Jonathan Metcalf
Art Director Bryn Walls

First published in Great Britain in 2007 by
Dorling Kindersley Limited
80 Strand, London WC2R 0RL
A Penguin Company

2 4 6 8 10 9 7 5 3 1

A CIP catalogue record for this book
is available from the British Library.

ISBN 978 1 40531 767 2

Printed and bound in China by
Hung Hing Offset Printing Company Ltd

Discover more at
www.dk.com

CONTENTS

FOREWORD

by Captain Eric "Winkle" Brown CBE, DSC, AFC

Most people envy the ability of birds to fly, so the concept of an aeroplane was supremely evocative to the human imagination, and has resulted in a steady stream of creative designs that have grown in sophistication as time has advanced.

The history of this mechanical evolution is mirrored in the 150 aircraft that form the subject of this book, and they have been chosen with great skill to give a comprehensive understanding of the incredible scope of aviation.

Once you have succumbed to the charismatic attraction of flight, as I did from an early age, your interest will grow into enthusiasm and possibly even addiction of a healthy sort.

Flying offers a freedom from "the surly bonds of earth" and an exhilarating *joie de vivre*. As well as giving great pleasure, it can also provide challenges, such as adverse weather or mechanical failure, to both the private and professional pilot; to the military and the test pilot, the challenges are much more demanding, as indeed they were for the early pioneers of flight.

I was fortunate to be around in the "Golden Age" of aviation (1930s–60s) when aesthetically beautiful aircraft such as the Supermarine S.6B of Schneider Trophy fame, Supermarine Spitfire, de Havilland Mosquito, Lockheed Constellation, Hawker Hunter, and Concorde graced the skies. There were also the "dogs", which were tricky to fly, such as the Granville Gee Bee racer, Messerschmitt Me163 rocket interceptor, and Northrop XB-49 flying wing.

I have flown 487 different types of aircraft in my time – according to the *Guinness Book of Records*, more than anyone else in history – and those listed in this book positively make my mouth water.

I shall enjoy reliving in memory the experience of actually flying some 40 of them, in particular the Gloster-Whittle E.28/39, Britain's first jet-propelled aeroplane.

I was involved with the flight-testing of that historic aircraft in 1944, and it opened up a whole new regime of flight. The first thing that struck me, after previously flying only propeller aeroplanes, was the E.28/39's magnificent all-round view from the cockpit, particularly straight ahead.

In spite of having more engine instruments than flight instruments – remember this was really a flying test-bed for the revolutionary jet engine – it was a confidence-generating cockpit, like that of the Avro Lancaster and Lockheed Martin F-16.

During take-off, acceleration was sluggish (as it was in all early jets), but the absence of noise and vibration was unexpectedly delightful and, once airborne, the build-up in speed was breathtaking.

Aviation has made fantastic progress since the Wright brothers first flew in 1903. This book illustrates and describes key aircraft that have contributed to that progress, and includes the phenomenal North American X-15, the Lockheed SR-71 Blackbird, and the Anglo-French Concorde. All are sheer magic...

Eric Brown

The conquest of the air was, without doubt, man's greatest achievement. For centuries heavier-than-air-flight had been deemed impossible, yet now problems were confronted and overcome: within a comparatively brief time span the aeroplane became the marvel of the new 20th century. Private individuals and governments invested fortunes in an assortment of occasionally bizarre "flying machines", often to discover that their investment had been wasted. But although the quest for powered flight attracted its fair share of charlatans and hare-brained inventors, there were also devoted pioneers, struggling on small incomes, yet sustained by heartfelt convictions and enthusiasm. Once practical aeroplanes began to appear in significant numbers, early flying meetings and competitions generated tremendous excitement, attracting spectators in their thousands. Pilots became heroes overnight, and any aviator making an emergency descent in a remote, apparently deserted field soon found himself surrounded by a swarm of curious, goggle-eyed locals.

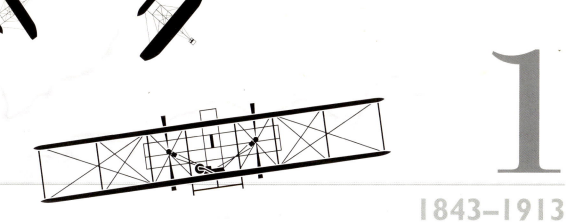

1

1843–1913

IT IS UTTER NONSENSE TO BELIEVE FLYING MACHINES WILL EVER WORK

HENSON'S AERIAL STEAM CARRIAGE

In the mid-1800s the belief in flight without the assistance of a balloon was dismissed as completely mad. So when Somerset lace manufacturer William Samuel Henson floated a bold scheme to found the world's first intercontinental airline in 1843, he faced considerable ridicule.

Formed with his friend John Stringfellow, the Aerial Transit Company was intended "for conveying letters, goods and passengers from place to place" aboard a steam-powered airliner. To tempt financial backers, fanciful engravings were published in various magazines depicting this splendid machine soaring above the Egyptian pyramids and other exotic locations.

The fatal flaw in Henson's imaginative project was that his Aerial Steam Carriage existed only on the drawing board – and if it had been built, would never have flown. No steam engine could have been at once light enough and powerful enough to lift the aircraft and its passengers into flight. And yet the Aerial Steam Carriage was an amazingly prophetic design.

It was a monoplane, its wire-braced wing formed by main spars and ribs covered with "strong oiled silk". The steam engine drove two pusher propellers on the wing's trailing edge. The pilot, accommodated with the passengers in an enclosed nacelle, was to control the aircraft via a moveable tailplane and rudder.

Unable to raise the necessary cash, Henson soon abandoned his aviation projects. But the seeds of a great idea had been sown.

"Heavier-than-air flying machines are impossible."

LORD KELVIN, PRESIDENT, ROYAL SOCIETY, 1895

SPECIFICATION

POWERPLANT 1 x 25–30-hp 2-cylinder Henson steam engine

WINGSPAN 45.7m (50ft)

WING AREA 418.sq m (4,500sq ft)

LENGTH Approx 25.8m (84ft 9in)

GROSS WEIGHT Approx 1,360kg (3,000lb)

CRUISING SPEED Debatable

RANGE Intercontinental

ACCOMMODATION 1 pilot, passengers, cargo

FIRST FLIGHT Unbuilt project

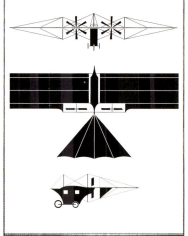

ALTHOUGH IT NEVER FLEW, THE DESIGN OF THE FANCIFUL AERIAL STEAM CARRIAGE WAS AHEAD OF ITS TIME

CAYLEY'S GLIDER HAD A BOAT-LIKE FUSELAGE AND AN UNDERCARRIAGE SPORTING INGENIOUS, TENSION-SPOKED WHEELS

CAYLEY GLIDER

The first heavier-than-air flying machines capable of carrying a man were the work of Yorkshire landowner Sir George Cayley. An amateur inventor of genius, Cayley devoted much of his life to investigating flight and testing model and full-size gliders.

Since these experiments were carried out in the privacy of his estate at Brompton Hall, details of his achievements are hard to establish. In 1849 a ten-year-old boy apparently made a brief ascent in a Cayley triplane. Four years later his terrified coachman was a reluctant passenger in another glider: the coachman is said to have quit his job on the spot, roundly declaring that he was "hired to drive, not to fly".

The glider shown here is a design Cayley published in 1852. Confusingly described as a "Governable Parachute", it had a short-span sail-wing similar to those now used in certain hang-gliders. The occupant, seated in a boat-like fuselage beneath the wing, controlled the craft through the "influencer": this was a combined rudder and elevator operated by a tiller. The glider's undercarriage used tension-spoked wheels, another of the baronet's ingenious inventions.

Cayley intended to have the craft taken aloft beneath a balloon and then released into a long, gliding descent. Sadly, when he died in 1857 the glider remained unbuilt.

In the 1970s, however, a full-size likeness was constructed, faithfully following Cayley's description. It successfully flew under tow across the valley at Brompton Dale, where the inventor had lived and worked.

"Flying is within our grasp. We have naught to do but take it."

CHARLES F. DURYEA, SPEAKING AT THE THIRD INTERNATIONAL
CONFERENCE ON AERONAUTICS, 1894

SPECIFICATION

POWERPLANT None

WING AREA 43.4sq m (467sq ft)

EMPTY WEIGHT Approx 68kg (150lb)

ACCOMMODATION 1 pilot

FIRST FLIGHT Unbuilt

MAXIM MULTIPLANE

In the 1890s English-domiciled American millionaire Hiram Maxim was in the forefront of inventors convinced that the key to flight was engine power. He spent £20,000 – a substantial part of the fortune he had made out of the Maxim machine-gun – building a massive 8,000lb aircraft.

With its welded steel-tube airframe and biplane wings spanning over 100ft, this behemoth was powered by two steam engines driving two pusher propellers, each 17ft 10in in diameter. There were fore and aft elevators for control in the vertical plane, while turning was to be achieved by varying the power delivered to each of the propellers.

Maxim did not initially intend the aircraft to be flown – if it had risen freely it would certainly have crashed. Instead, it was mounted on a track, with restraining rails to prevent it lifting more than 2ft into the air.

On 31 July 1894, at Baldwyn's Park in Kent, the mighty machine was prepared for a test run. Accelerating to 42mph, it lifted until all of its outrigger wheels were engaged on the restraining rails. But disaster soon struck. An axle failed, a restraining rail broke, and the machine crashed to a halt. No further "flights" were attempted.

"The great bird will take its first flight…filling the world with amazement and all records with its fame, and it will bring eternal glory to the nest where it was born."

LEONARDO DA VINCI, RENAISSANCE ARTIST

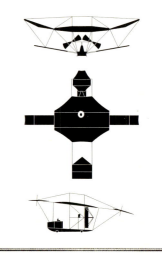

SPECIFICATION

POWERPLANT 2 x 180-hp Maxim steam engines

WINGSPAN 31.7m (104ft)

WING/ELEVATOR AREA 371.6sq m (4,000sq ft)

LENGTH Approx 28.9m (95ft)

GROSS WEIGHT 3,630kg (8,000lb)

LIFTING SPEED Approx 64km/h (40mph)

ACCOMMODATION 4 crew

FIRST TEST 31 July 1894

INTENDED NOT TO FLY BUT TO PROVE THE CONCEPT OF POWERED FLIGHT, THE MULTIPLANE RAN ALONG SPECIALLY DESIGNED TRACKS

This fanciful vision of aviation in 2012 shows a chauffeur-driven aeroplane for the wealthy, and appeared on an advertising postcard issued by *Chocolat Lombart* of Paris in the early 20th century. Few guessed then how far aviation would advance in 100 years.

LILIENTHAL'S NO.11 HANG-GLIDER WAS CONTROLLED BY SIMPLY SWINGING THE BODY BACK AND FORTH

LILIENTHAL NO.11 HANG-GLIDER

In the early 1890s German engineer Otto Lilienthal was the only person in the world flying with wings. Crowds flocked to witness his flight experiments in the Berlin suburb of Lichterfelde, where he had built an artificial hill from which to take off. He would stride down into the wind until borne aloft by his bird-like wings. Swinging from side to side or back and forth to maintain balance, he sometimes flew for several hundred metres before returning to earth.

This riveting spectacle smacked more of the circus than of science, yet Lilienthal was a serious researcher, convinced that the only way to understand flight was "by actual flying experiments". His flight trials received worldwide publicity, attracting the attention,

among others, of Wilbur and Orville Wright in Dayton, Ohio.

Lilienthal's most reliable glider was the eleventh that he designed. Called the *Normal-Segelapparat* ("standard sailing machine"), it was a simple willow structure covered with English shirting material. In this hang-glider Lilienthal achieved flights of up to 820ft.

He sold or presented eight No. 11s to other would-be experimenters, some of whom baulked at entrusting their lives to such a flimsy structure. It was while flying his No. 11, on 9 August 1896, that Lilienthal met his death. The glider was gusted to a halt, stalled, and side-slipped into the ground. Tragically, Lilienthal's spine was broken and he died the following day.

> *"We returned home, after these experiments, with the conviction that sailing flight was not the exclusive prerogative of birds."*
>
> OTTO LILIENTHAL, AVIATION PIONEER

SPECIFICATION

POWERPLANT None

WINGSPAN 7m (23ft)

WING AREA 14sq m (151sq ft)

LENGTH 5m (16ft 5in)

EMPTY WEIGHT 20kg (44lb)

ACCOMMODATION 1 pilot

FIRST FLIGHT 1894

CHANUTE BIPLANE GLIDER

In the summer of 1896 French-born American Octave Chanute, a wealthy railroad engineer who had published a history of flight experiments, camped out on the windswept shore of Lake Michigan, determined to turn his theory into practice. In his mid-60s, Chanute was too old to fly himself, but he was accompanied by young engineer Augustus Moore Herring, who served as his assistant and test pilot.

The biplane glider was the second machine Chanute and Herring tested that summer, and it was by far the most successful. Its outstanding feature was the use of vertical struts and wire cross-bracing to make the wing structure a rigid, open "box-girder". Cleverly adapted by Chanute from the Pratt truss used in railway bridges, this system combined strength and lightness so effectively that it has remained standard for biplanes ever since.

The pilot hung on parallel bars under his armpits, controlling the glider by moving his body. Gliding down sandhills, Augustus Herring flew for up to 253ft in the machine's first trials; in a fresh wind on 11 September 1896 he succeeded in covering 359ft in 14 seconds. The biplane was so safe that, the following year, Herring allowed journalists to sample the joys of gliding flight.

"All agreed that the sensation of coasting on the air was delightful."

OCTAVE CHANUTE, AVIATION PIONEER

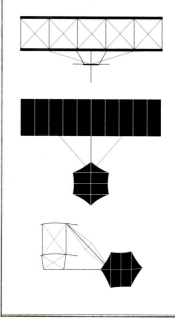

SPECIFICATION

POWERPLANT None

WINGSPAN 4.8m (16ft)

WING AREA 12.5sq m (135sq ft)

EMPTY WEIGHT 14kg (31lb)

ACCOMMODATION 1 pilot

FIRST FLIGHT August 1896

THE OUTSTANDING FEATURE OF CHANUTE'S GLIDER WAS ITS WING STRUCTURE, A RIGID, OPEN "BOX-GIRDER" STILL USED TODAY

ADER MODELLED HIS CURIOUS STEAM-POWERED MONOPLANE ON THE BAT

ADER AVION III

Whenever a sceptic wants to cast doubt on the Wright brothers' claim to be "first to fly", he is likely to cite the experiments of French engineer Clément Ader. Where most aviation pioneers studied the flight of birds, Ader perversely modelled his flying machines on bats. His weirdly gothic steam-powered monoplanes were sufficiently impressive to attract financial backing from the French army, but whether they actually flew remains open to doubt.

Ader's first machine, the *Eole* of 1890, has been credited with the first powered take-off; however, there is no hard evidence to back the claim. His second was Avion III (the intervening Avion II being abandoned as a failure). Its two 20-hp steam engines each drove a propeller with four bamboo blades resembling giant feathers. Its only controls were a painfully slow method of swinging the wings fore and aft horizontally, a fabric rudder operated by pedals that also turned the rear undercarriage wheel, and a differential speed device for the propellers.

On its first trial, conducted on a circular track, Avion III remained stubbornly earthbound. Two days later, on its second trial, the rear wheel apparently lifted but the aircraft was then wrecked by a gust of wind. It was never tested again.

However, in 1906 Ader suddenly claimed to have made a flight of 984ft on the machine's second outing; the evidence suggests that it never got off the ground.

SPECIFICATION

POWERPLANT 2 x 20-hp Ader steam engines with one boiler

WINGSPAN 16m (52ft 6in)

WING AREA 56sq m (603sq ft)

GROSS WEIGHT Approx 400kg (882lb)

ACCOMMODATION 1 pilot

FIRST FLIGHT ATTEMPT 12 October 1897

"Caution: Cape does not enable user to fly."

BATMAN COSTUME WARNING LABEL, WAL-MART

PILCHER TRIPLANE

Flight pioneer Percy Pilcher is one of Britain's unsung heroes. But for a fatal accident it is possible that he, rather than the celebrated Wright brothers, might have solved the riddle of powered, controlled, heavier-than-air flight.

Inspired by Lilienthal, Pilcher built four gliders in 1895, the last of which, the *Hawk*, was the most successful. In 1897, working with engineer Walter Wilson, he decided to fit a small two-cylinder petrol engine in a glider for experiments with powered flight.

Influenced by Chanute, the new machine was designed as a triplane. The engine was to be mounted high at the front, with a long driveshaft to a two-bladed pusher propeller behind the wings. Pilcher would have had problems controlling this machine as he depended on body-swinging, and had yet to try other methods such as rudders or elevators. In the event, the control issue was never put to the test. A first attempt to fly the triplane was delayed when the engine's crankshaft broke.

Meanwhile, Pilcher went ahead with a demonstration of his glider, the *Hawk*, at Stanford Park, near Rugby, on 30 September 1899. Tragically, the craft suffered a structural failure during a towed flight from level ground, and Pilcher subseqently died of his injuries on 2 October. His triplane was never flown.

In 2003, however, a full-size reproduction flew successfully, happily demonstrating that the design was indeed practical.

"I am well convinced that 'Aerial Navigation' will form a most prominent feature in the progress of civilization."

SIR GEORGE CAYLEY, AVIATION PIONEER

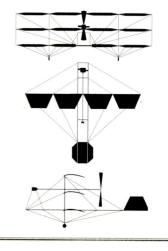

SPECIFICATION

POWERPLANT 1 × 4/5-hp Wilson & Pilcher 2-cylinder petrol engine

WINGSPAN 7m (23ft)

WING AREA 13.3sq m (144sq ft)

LENGTH 5.8m (19ft)

EMPTY WEIGHT 20–27kg (50–60lb)

FLYING SPEED Approx 48km/h (30mph)

ACCOMMODATION 1 pilot

FIRST FLIGHT Untested (reproduction: 29 August 2003)

PILCHER'S TRIPLANE WOULD HAVE BEEN DIFFICULT TO CONTROL, HAD IT FLOWN, AS IT WAS ENTIRELY STEERED BY BODY SWINGING

In this, the most famous aviation photograph ever taken, Orville Wright makes the world's first powered, controlled flight, lasting 12 seconds, in the Flyer I on 17 December 1903 at Kitty Hawk, North Carolina. His brother, Wilbur, looks on.

WRIGHT FLYER III

The Wright Flyer III was the world's first practical powered aeroplane, sturdy enough to withstand repeated flights and able to stay aloft for as long as its fuel lasted.

Through a remarkable mix of scientific inquiry and hands-on experimentation, the dauntless American brothers Wilbur and Orville Wright cracked the challenge of sustained, controlled, heavier-than-air flight. At Kill Devil Hills, North Carolina, on 17 December 1903, they proved that their Flyer could fly. But the longest of the four flights made on that momentous day lasted only 59 seconds. The brothers devoted the next two years to improving their machine. After making flights of up to five minutes with Flyer II in the summer of 1904, they built Flyer III during the winter of 1904–05.

Between June and October 1905 the Wrights made more than 40 flights near Dayton, Ohio, totalling some three hours. They mastered the art of turning in the air, banking, circling, and performing figures of eight. In the longest flight, on 5 October, Wilbur remained aloft for 38 minutes and 3 seconds, covering over 24 miles. Three years were to pass before anyone else produced a plane capable of a comparable performance.

"If you are looking for perfect safety...sit on a fence and watch the birds; but if you really wish to learn, you must mount the machine and become acquainted with its tricks by actual trial."

WILBUR WRIGHT, AVIATION PIONEER

SPECIFICATION

POWERPLANT 1 x 15–20-hp 4-cylinder Wright engine

WINGSPAN 12.3m (40ft 6in)

WING AREA 46.7sq m (503sq ft)

LENGTH 8.5m (28ft)

WEIGHT 322kg (710lb)

ENDURANCE Approx 40min

ACCOMMODATION 1 pilot

FIRST FLIGHT 23 June 1905

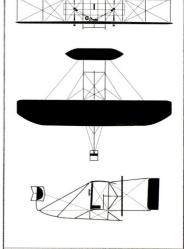

THE STURDY WRIGHT FLYER III WAS THE WORLD'S FIRST PRACTICAL POWERED AEROPLANE

CODY BRITISH ARMY AEROPLANE NO. I

The first powered aeroplane to fly in Britain was the brainchild of an expatriate American, S. F. "Cody". Born in Iowa as Samuel Franklin Cowdery, he had renamed himself after his gun-slinging hero, "Buffalo Bill" Cody. A flamboyant personality, Cowdery/Cody ran a Wild West show before moving to Britain in 1896 and developing an interest in flight.

He was employed by the British Army after making a man-carrying kite that could be used as an airborne observation post. In late 1907, with the support of Colonel Capper, Superintendent of the Army Balloon Factory at Farnborough, Hampshire, Cody embarked on the design and construction of a powered aircraft. British Army Aeroplane No. 1 was unveiled in mid-September 1908.

A large biplane, it was powered by a 50-hp Antoinette engine driving a pair of pusher propellers through a belt drive. After a series of tests on the ground, the first flight was made on the morning of 16 October 1908 on Farnborough Common.

Cody flew for 1,390ft before crashing while trying to avoid some troublesome trees. However, the War Office found aviation too expensive, and Cody's contract was abruptly terminated in 1909.

He continued to build and fly aeroplanes until 1913, when he was killed piloting one of his machines that broke up in flight.

"There are two critical points in every aerial flight – its beginning and its end."

ALEXANDER GRAHAM BELL, SCIENTIST

SPECIFICATION

POWERPLANT I × 50-hp Antoinette engine

WINGSPAN 15.8m (52ft)

WING AREA 80sq m (861¼ sq ft)

LENGTH 9.54m (31ft 3in)

GROSS WEIGHT 1,044kg (2,301lb)

FLYING SPEED 40–48km/h (25–30mph)

ACCOMMODATION I crew

FIRST FLIGHT 16 October 1908

THE CODY BRITISH ARMY AEROPLANE NO. 1, A LARGE BIPLANE, WAS THE FIRST POWERED AIRCRAFT TO FLY IN BRITAIN

SANTOS-DUMONT DEMOISELLE

Alberto Santos-Dumont's delicate Demoiselle ("damselfly") monoplane was the true ancestor of all ultralights. A Brazilian-born Parisian dandy, Santos-Dumont was renowned for airship flights before he turned to creating heavier-than-air machines in 1905.

His public demonstration flights in his first powered aircraft during October 1906 – the first in Europe – caused a sensation. But this was a clumsy box-kite biplane that, at best, managed only a hop of 722ft. The elegant Demoiselle series was altogether more successful. The prototype No. 19, produced in late 1907, managed only three short flights, but the Demoiselle was reborn in 1908-09 as the more sturdy No. 20.

Sitting beneath the high wing, with the engine above his head, the pilot had a lever connected to his jacket, operating a wing-warping apparatus; by moving his body, he could twist the wingtips for lateral control.

Light and sensitive, the Demoiselle was flyable only in the calmest weather and was so small that few people, other than the diminutive Santos-Dumont, could pilot it. Yet some 10 or 15 were sold, including the No. 21 and larger No. 22 models.

"Suddenly Santos-Dumont points the end of the machine skyward, and the wheels...leave the soil... The whole crowd is stirred. Santos-Dumont seems to fly like some immense bird in a fairy tale."

LE FIGARO REPORTING ON EUROPE'S FIRST PUBLIC POWERED FLIGHT

SPECIFICATION

POWERPLANT 1 × 35-hp 2-cylinder Dutheil-Chalmers engine

WINGSPAN 5m (16ft 8¾in)

WING AREA 10.2sq m (110 sq ft)

LENGTH 8m (26ft 3in)

GROSS WEIGHT 143kg (315lb)

SPEED 90km/h (56mph)

ACCOMMODATION 1 pilot

FIRST FLIGHT 6 March 1909

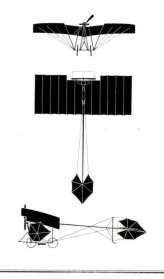

THE PILOT SAT BENEATH THE DEMOISELLE'S WING, ROCKING HIS BODY TO ACHIEVE LATERAL CONTROL

BLÉRIOT'S TYPE XI MONOPLANE MADE HISTORY BY SUCCESSFULLY COMPLETING THE FIRST CROSS-CHANNEL FLIGHT IN 1909

BLÉRIOT XI

French aviation pioneer Louis Blériot's Type XI monoplane won its place in the history books by making the first cross-Channel flight from France to England on 25 July 1909. Taking off from Les Baraques near Calais, Blériot flew for just over half an hour to land near Dover Castle in Kent and claim a £1,000 prize offered by newspaper magnate Lord Northcliffe.

A seriously accident-prone flight enthusiast, Blériot was fortunate to have survived testing the extraordinary variety of flying machines he had constructed over the preceding four years. The Type XI appeared in December 1908, probably created with input from brilliant young French engineer Raymond Saulnier. The following April it was fitted with an Anzani engine – not a hefty power source but just adequate for flying the Channel.

Blériot had already made many flights of up to 50 minutes duration in this simple, practical machine but his cross-Channel excursion definitively proved its worth.

Naturally, wealthy sportsmen queued up to buy the aeroplane that had performed such an historic feat, and armies soon followed suit. Produced in substantial numbers, the Type XI made Blériot's fortune. Fitted with a more powerful engine, it continued in service into the early years of World War I.

"I headed for this white mountain…A break in the coast appeared to my right, just before Dover Castle. I was madly happy. I headed for it. I rushed for it. I was above ground!"

LOUIS BLÉRIOT, RECALLING HIS CROSS-CHANNEL FEAT

SPECIFICATION

POWERPLANT 1 × 25-hp 3-cylinder Anzani engine

WINGSPAN 7.8m (25ft 7in)

WING AREA 14sq m (150¾sq ft)

LENGTH 8m (26ft 3in)

GROSS WEIGHT 300kg (661lb)

SPEED: APPROX 76km/h (47mph)

ACCOMMODATION 1 pilot

FIRST FLIGHT 23 January 1909

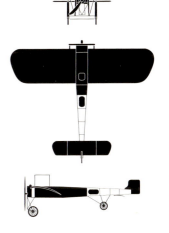

British aviator Claude Grahame-White prepares for his second attempt to win the *Daily Mail* £10,000 prize for a flight from London to Manchester. His Farman biplane is seen surrounded by spectators at Wormwood Scrubbs, West London, on 27 April 1910.

CURTISS REIMS RACER

In August 1909 most of the adventurous pioneers then flying aeroplanes gathered at Reims in France for the world's first air show. The sole American present was Glenn Curtiss. His Reims Racer, the second aeroplane he had built, was a small, light pusher biplane built for speed

Its pilot sat over the leading edge of the lower wing, using a wheel-topped stick-control to operate the rudder and elevator, which was at the forward end of the machine. He used a shoulder yoke to work the ailerons fitted between the upper and lower wingtips.

Pitted in the Reims speed contests against the much-fancied Blériot and Antionette monoplanes, Curtiss performed outstandingly. On 28 August his mount proved fastest over the 20km distance, reaching 47mph to win the Gordon Bennett Cup. The following day he took the 10,000-franc speed prize, averaging 46½mph over 30km. The Curtiss pusher was triumphantly established as a premier aircraft type.

"When they saw me circle the church spire, the people went wild. The next day, papers reported of trams stopping... and the sick crawling to the windows..."

ANTON FOKKER, AVIATOR, RECALLING AN EARLY FLIGHT

SMALL AND LIGHT, THE REIMS RACER WAS DESIGNED FOR SPEED

SPECIFICATION

POWERPLANT 1 × 50-hp Curtiss 8-cylinder engine

WINGSPAN 8m (26ft 3in)

WING AREA 10.9sq m (118sq ft)

LENGTH 9.2m (30ft 4in)

GROSS WEIGHT 317kg (700lb)

SPEED 76km/h (47mph)

ACCOMMODATION 1 pilot, 1 passenger

FIRST FLIGHT August 1909

FARMAN III BIPLANE

The slow but dependable Farman III was the classic pre-World War I biplane, sold around the world. Its creator, Henry (or Henri) Farman, was of English parentage but lived all his life in France.

He began his aviation career flying a Voisin box-kite biplane. After modifying this machine extensively, including fitting ailerons, he used it to make the world's first true cross-country flight, a 20-minute journey from Bouy to Reims, on 30 October 1908.

Farman began producing his own machines after the Voisin company annoyed him by selling an aircraft he had ordered to another client. The Farman III was his first original design. It had downward-moving ailerons for lateral control and was initially powered by a 50-hp Vivinus engine.

During the famous Reims flying meeting in August 1909 Farman replaced the Vivinus with a Gnome rotary engine – an innovative aero-engine concept in which the cylinders revolved with the propeller. Light and comparatively reliable, the Gnome ensured that Farman's aircraft became one of the Reims meeting's star performers. While not a contender for speed records, it won the distance prize by covering 180km in just over three hours continuous flight.

Farman's aircraft manufacturing business flourished. His biplanes featured in flying meetings all over the world, making the first flights in Brazil, China, and Vietnam in 1910. Because they were relatively safe and easy to fly, descendants of the III were adopted as a standard military training aircraft.

"To invent an airplane is nothing. To build one is something. To fly is everything."

OTTO LILIENTHAL, AVIATION PIONEER

SPECIFICATION

POWERPLANT 1 x 50-hp 7-cylinder Gnome rotary engine

WINGSPAN 10m (32¾ft)

WING AREA 40sq m (430½ sq ft)

LENGTH 12m (39¼ft)

GROSS WEIGHT 550kg (1,213lb)

SPEED 59km/h (37mph)

ACCOMMODATION 1 pilot, 1 passenger

FIRST FLIGHT 6 April 1909 (Vivinus engine)

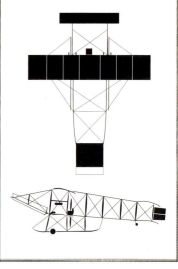

EASY TO FLY AND WITH A GOOD REPUTATION FOR SAFETY, THE FARMAN III WAS THE CLASSIC PRE-WORLD WAR I BIPLANE

THE VOISIN BIPLANE RELIED ON RUDDER CONTROL, SO TURNS HAD TO BE FLAT AND WIDE TO AVOID SIDESLIPPING INTO THE GROUND

VOISIN BIPLANE

French brothers Gabriel and Charles Voisin were Europe's first commercial aeroplane manufacturers, making aircraft for customers as early as 1906. By 1909 the typical aircraft emerging from their Paris factory was a large pusher biplane based on the principle of the box-kite, as developed by Australian Lawrence Hargrave.

Voisin biplanes had an elevator mounted on the front of the fabric-covered nacelle that housed the pilot and engine, and a rudder inside the box-like tail structure.

However, the Voisin brothers did not understand the need for ailerons for lateral control, assuming that turns could be made on rudder alone. This was indeed possible, but the pilot had to exercise great caution, making flat, wide turns to avoid the aircraft sideslipping into the ground.

Voisin designs emphasized stability above all else, so the struts between the wings and tailplanes were covered by fabric "curtains" to provide stabilizing side areas. A strong and heavy tubular steel undercarriage with spiral springs helped withstand the rough aerodrome surfaces often encountered in the early days of flying. A variety of engines were installed, according to customers' requirements.

A number of famous flight pioneers, including Léon Delagrange and Henry Farman, bought Voisin biplanes and flew them successfully, often modifying them in the process. But these ungainly, cumbersome aircraft quickly became outdated.

"High spirits they had: gravity they flouted."

CECIL DAY LEWIS, POET

SPECIFICATION

POWERPLANT 1 × 60-hp ENV 8-cylinder engine

WINGSPAN 10m (32ft 10in)

WING AREA 40sq m (430½sq ft)

LENGTH 12m (39ft 4in)

GROSS WEIGHT 600kg (1,320lb)

SPEED 55km/h (34mph)

ACCOMMODATION 1 pilot, 1 passenger

FIRST TAKE-OFF (Voisin-Delagrange I of 1907, first of the line): 16 March 1907

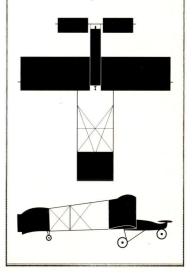

FABRE HYDRAVION

Looking at aeroplanes from the pioneering era of flight, it sometimes seems almost incredible that such machines actually flew. The freakish Hydravion is certainly a case in point. Yet this odd-looking aircraft enjoys the distinction of being the first seaplane to make a successful flight – and it did so with a pilot who had never flown before.

Frenchman Henri Fabre, whose family were shipowners, designed and built the Hydravion during 1909–10 after studying the work of other French pioneers. One of the first aircraft to be powered by the 50-hp 7-cylinder Gnome rotary engine, it had the canard layout favoured by the Wright brothers – that is,

with the tail at the front rather than at the back. The rear-mounted engine drove a two-blade propeller. The fuselage simply comprised two boxed-in lattice girders, one above the other. Perched in a most exposed position halfway along the upper girder, the pilot controlled the aircraft using wing warping and a tiller linked to the twin rudders. The machine was supported on three floats.

Its maiden flight was made on 28 March 1910. The next day, on Henri Fabre's fifth flight, he covered some 3¾ miles. The Hydravion was modified after an accident the following May, but it continued to be flown until March 1911.

"I've never known an industry that can get into people's blood the way aviation does."

ROBERT SIX, FOUNDER OF CONTINENTAL AIRLINES

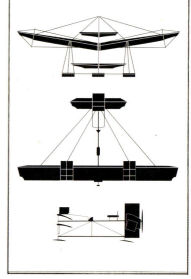

SPECIFICATION

POWERPLANT 1 x 50-hp 7-cylinder Gnome rotary engine

WINGSPAN 14m (45ft 11in)

WING AREA 17sq m (1,83sq ft)

LENGTH 8.5m (27ft 10½in)

GROSS WEIGHT 475kg (1,047lb)

SPEED 88km/h (55mph)

ACCOMMODATION 1 pilot

FIRST FLIGHT 28 March 1910

THE BIZARRE-LOOKING HYDRAVION FROM FRANCE WAS THE FIRST SEAPLANE TO FLY SUCCESSFULLY

ANTOINETTE MONOBLOC

French aviation pioneers often favoured elegance and ingenuity over plain practicality. The *Société Antoinette* produced a series of aesthetically satisfying, technically advanced monoplanes designed by engineer and former artist Léon Levavasseur. Sadly, they did not always fulfil their promise.

The Antoinette IV, the company's first monoplane, famously failed to cross the Channel in July 1909, ditching instead in the sea. It was the pilot on that occasion, wealthy big-game hunter Hubert Latham, who laid down the specification for the Antoinette Monobloc three-seater,

shown here. In 1911 it was entered into the *Concours Militaire*, an Army competition to evaluate potential military aeroplanes.

Streamlined to maximize performance, the wooden wing was braced internally; the warp control wires, used for lateral control, were also run inside the wing. Long "petticoats" enclosed the main wheels, and the crew compartment was covered by a transparent fairing, so that occupants entered via a door under the fuselage. Alas, for all its streamlined ingenuity, the Monobloc proved underpowered for its weight, and was ultimately a non-flyer.

> *"The danger? But danger is one of the attractions of flight."*
>
> JEAN CONNEAU, PIONEER AVIATOR

ALTHOUGH THE ANTOINETTE MONOBLOC WAS A REVOLUTIONARY, FORWARD-LOOKING DESIGN, IT WAS TOO HEAVY TO FLY SUCCESSFULLY

SPECIFICATION

POWERPLANT 1 × 60-hp 8-cylinder Antoinette engine

WINGSPAN 15.9m (52ft 2in)

WING AREA 56sqm (602¾sq ft)

LENGTH 11.5m (37ft 9in)

GROSS WEIGHT 1,350kg (2,976lb)

ACCOMMODATION 1 pilot, 2 crew

FIRST FLIGHT Not flown

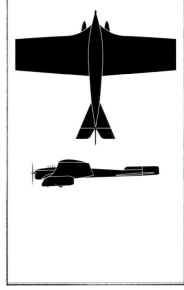

PAULHAN-TATIN AERO-TORPILLE

One of the more conspicuous machines at the French military aeroplane trials in October 1911 was the Paulhan-Tatin Aero-Torpille (aero-torpedo). It was designed by veteran flight experimenter Victor Tatin, and built by Louis Paulhan, then France's most famous young aviator.

This happy collaboration of youth and age produced a sleek, streamlined monoplane that was in some ways ahead of its time. The 50-hp Gnome engine was completely enclosed in the fuselage, behind the cockpit, and cooled by air cunningly admitted through louvres in the fuselage sides.

Power was transmitted through a 20ft-long shaft to a two-bladed propeller in the extreme tail. The fuselage was actually a square-section girder structure, faired to a circular cross-section with fabric-covered, light, wooden formers.

To provide lateral stability, the outer portions of the aeroplane's wings were curved gracefully upwards. The undercarriage, by contrast, simply comprised a pair of wheels on an axle attached to two curved wooden struts that acted as shock absorbers. A tall tailskid protected the propeller against contact with the ground.

The Aero-Torpille was reportedly capable of speeds as high as 88mph, but it proved a difficult machine to control. This may go some way to explaining why such a striking and innovative aeroplane vanished from the scene after a notably brief existence.

"The man who flies an airplane…must believe in the unseen."

RICHARD BACH, AUTHOR

SPECIFICATION

POWERPLANT 1 × 50-hp 7-cylinder Gnome rotary engine

WINGSPAN 8.5m (28ft)

WING AREA 12.5sq m (134½sq ft)

LENGTH 8.2m (27ft)

EMPTY WEIGHT 360kg (793½lb)

SPEED 141km/h (88mph)

ACCOMMODATION 1 pilot

FIRST FLIGHT late 1911

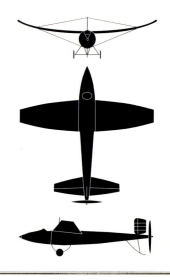

ALTHOUGH SLEEK, FAST, AND AHEAD OF ITS TIME, THE AERO-TORPILLE MONOPLANE WAS DIFFICULT TO CONTROL

THE B.E.2's MAJOR WEAKNESS WAS ITS STABILITY; MANOEUVRABILITY WAS SACRIFICED, MAKING IT VULNERABLE TO ENEMY ATTACK

ROYAL AIRCRAFT FACTORY B.E.2

A military two-seater, the B.E.2 had the misfortune to become one of the most maligned aircraft of World War I. Yet when the prototype first appeared, in February 1912, its performance was judged to be little short of impressive.

The B.E.2 was designed by Geoffrey de Havilland at the Royal Aircraft Factory, Farnborough, to meet the newly formed Royal Flying Corps' need for a reconnaissance aircraft to operate in liaison with ground forces. Because it was "government-built", it was not officially allowed to compete in the military trials held in the summer of 1912; however, flown for demonstration purposes only, it proceeded to outshine most of the aircraft entered by private constructors. Put out to various private companies for manufacture, the B.E.2 then entered service with the Royal Flying Corps Military Wing.

Certainly, it had solid virtues: it was more dependable than most aircraft of the period, and its stability made it an excellent platform for photographing enemy positions.

Unfortunately, its very stability ensured that it was also sluggish, and B.E.2s proved easy meat for agile enemy fighters. Neither did it help that the aircraft's gun was entrusted to the observer, who sat in front of the pilot: surrounded by struts and wires, it was near impossible for him to bring his gun to bear on an attacker.

The B.E.2c version of the aircraft was kept in frontline service for far too long, leading it to be accurately denounced as "a reckless waste of human life".

"It seems to me that the conquest of the air is the only major task for our generation."

T.E. LAWRENCE, BRITISH SOLDIER AND AUTHOR

SPECIFICATION

POWERPLANT 1 × 70-hp Renault engine

WINGSPAN 11.3m (36ft 11in)

WING AREA 34.9sq m (376sq ft)

LENGTH 8.9m (29ft 6½in)

GROSS WEIGHT 726kg (1,600lb)

MAXIMUM SPEED 127km/h (70mph)

ENDURANCE 3hr

ACCOMMODATION 2 crew

FIRST FLIGHT 1 February 1912

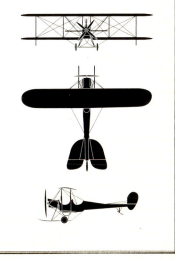

DEPERDUSSIN SEAPLANE RACER

Founded in 1910, French businessman Armand Deperdussin's company was famed for its racing monoplanes, which were then the fastest aeroplanes in the world.

The key to their success was the use of the monocoque ("single shell") method for building a light yet strong fuselage. Originally devised by Swedish engineer Ruchonnet, the technique was adopted by Deperdussin's designer, Louis Béchereau, in 1911. Layers of plywood were laid on a mould to create a shell requiring minimal internal reinforcement. The resulting smooth, streamlined structure, fitted with the most powerful available engines, took the air racing world by storm.

The first Deperdussin racer, fitted with a 140-hp engine, won the 1912 Gordon Bennett Trophy race in Chicago, Illinois, at 108.18mph. The floatplane version, shown here, was entered for the first Schneider Trophy contest for seaplanes, held in April 1913 at Monaco.

On 7 April 1913 pilot Maurice Prévost pancaked the seaplane on to the water, breaking its rear fuselage; it was quickly repaired and eight days later, on 15 April, Prévost won the trophy. He averaged only 61mph for the 28 laps, but his competitors had all retired or been eliminated.

"Cloud flying requires practice…In the very early days of aviation,…I emerged from a cloud upside down, much to my discomfort, as I didn't know how to get right way up again. I found out somehow, or I wouldn't be writing this."

CHARLES RUMNEY SAMSON, AUTHOR,
WRITING IN *A FLIGHT FROM CAIRO TO CAPE TOWN AND BACK*

SPECIFICATION

POWERPLANT 1 x 160-hp 14-cylinder Gnome rotary engine

WINGSPAN 8.9m (29ft 4in)

WING AREA 9sq m (96¾sq ft)

LENGTH 5.7m (18ft 10in)

GROSS WEIGHT 400kg (882lb)

MAXIMUM SPEED 105km/h (65mph)

ACCOMMODATION 1 pilot

FIRST FLIGHT 1913

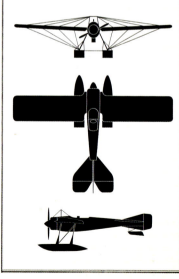

THEIR STREAMLINED MONOCOCQUE CONSTRUCTION AND POWERFUL ENGINES MADE DEPERDUSSIN'S AEROPLANES FAMOUSLY FAST

This early colour photograph shows
a German Grade monoplane of 1912,
with its creator standing alongside.
As in the smaller French Demoiselle,
the pilot sat beneath the wings, exposed
to the blast from the propeller.

THE RUMPLER TAUBE WAS TOO SLOW AND FLIMSY TO SURVIVE LONG INTO WORLD WAR I AND SOON WENT OUT OF SERVICE

RUMPLER TAUBE

Bird-like Taube ("dove") monoplanes proliferated in Germany and Austria before 1914, meeting military demand for a stable two-seater reconnaissance machine.

The distinctive design was the work of Austrian engineer Dr Igo Etrich. From his first glider in 1904, Etrich evolved the unique avian silhouette with its striking sweptback wingtips. Curiously, the wing shape was modelled not on birds but on the winged seed of the Zanonia, a native vine of Java.

The first Etrich Taube was flown in 1910, later models being used by the Turks in the 1913 Balkan War. Other manufacturers produced their own versions of the design, the foremost of these being the Rumpler Flugzeugwerke of Johannisthal, Berlin. At least 66 of the 1913 Rumpler 3C model, shown here, were bought by the German Army.

An odd feature the Rumpler version shared with most other Taubes was the external girder bracing beneath the wings, which must have caused a great deal of undesirable drag. Stable and pleasant to fly, Taubes performed useful reconnaissance work early in World War I. One German Taube even carried out the first air attack on a city, dropping five small bombs on Paris in August 1914.

"At first we will only skim the surface of the earth like young starlings, but soon, emboldened by practice and experiences, we will spring into the air with the impetuousness of the eagle."

JEAN-JACQUES ROUSSEAU, 18TH CENTURY PHILOSOPHER

SPECIFICATION

POWERPLANT 1 × 100-hp 6-cylinder Mercedes engine

WINGSPAN 14.3m (47ft 1in)

WING AREA Approx 34.8sq m (375sq ft)

LENGTH 9.8m (32ft 4in)

GROSS WEIGHT 870kg (1,918lb)

MAXIMUM SPEED 116km/h (72mph)

ACCOMMODATION 2 crew

FIRST FLIGHT 1913

RADLEY-ENGLAND WATERPLANE

Designed and built in Britain by James Radley and Eric Gordon England, the Waterplane was the world's first tri-motor aeroplane. Its three 50-hp rotary engines were mounted between the wings. Each engine had its own controls and an independent chain drive linking it to the propeller shaft above. Together the engines drove a large four-bladed pusher propeller.

The aircraft was sizeable for its day, carrying five passengers in its twin floats, or hulls. The pilot occupied the front seat in the starboard float, with two passengers behind him. Mounted above the floats was a biplane superstructure, with a tailplane and twin rudders carried on booms.

In initial tests as a landplane, with a temporary wheeled undercarriage, the aircraft proved an excellent flyer. Shifting to its intended element, the Waterplane was flown from the River Adur at Shoreham in Sussex and then from the sea at Brighton.

Disaster struck on 26 May 1913, when one of the floats hit an object on landing and was holed. The aircraft was rebuilt with clinker-built hulls and one 150-hp Sunbeam engine. However, the new engine proved troublesome and the aircraft never flew again.

> *"At that time [in the early 1900s], the chief engineer was almost always the chief test pilot as well. That had the fortunate result of eliminating poor engineering early in aviation."*
>
> IGOR SIKORSKY, AVIATION PIONEER

SPECIFICATION

POWERPLANT 3 × 50-hp 7-cylinder Gnome rotary engines

WINGSPAN 13.8m (45ft 4in)

WING AREA 46.9sq m (505sq ft)

LENGTH 8.8m (29ft 3in)

EMPTY WEIGHT Approx 635kg (1,400lb)

CRUISING SPEED 96km/h (60mph)

ENDURANCE 1½hr

ACCOMMODATION 1 pilot, 5 passengers

FIRST FLIGHT (AS A LANDPLANE) 9 or 10 April 1913

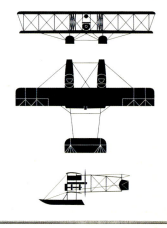

THE RADLEY-ENGLAND WATERPLANE WAS FIRST FLOWN AS A LANDPLANE WITH A TEMPORARY WHEELED UNDERCARRIAGE

DURING FLIGHT, PASSENGERS COULD ENJOY THE VIEW FROM THE OPEN BALCONY AT THE FRONT OF THE SIKORSKY GRAND

SIKORSKY BOLSHOI ("GRAND")

In 1912 Igor Sikorsky, chief engineer at the Russo-Baltic Wagon Works in St Petersburg embarked on the design and construction of the world's first four-engined aircraft. A huge machine by the standards of the time, it was appropriately named the "Bolshoi" ("Grand") – although sceptics, convinced that it could never fly, dubbed it the "Petersburg Duck".

Sikorsky proved them wrong on 10 May 1913, when the Grand made the first of many successful flights. Its performance improved further from July when the four engines, originally configured as two back-to-back tractor-and-pusher pairs, were rearranged in a row along the wing leading edge.

The aircraft's scale allowed Sikorsky to offer his passengers unprecedented comfort. A saloon was furnished with wicker chairs, a table, electric lights, curtains, and linoleum on the floor. At the rear were a wardrobe and washroom. During flight, hardy passengers could stroll on to an open balcony at the front of the aircraft to enjoy the view, while mechanics clambered out along the lower wing to tend the engines.

The Grand's brief but brilliant career was ended by a freak accident on 24 September 1913. The aircraft was on the ground when the engine from an aeroplane flying overhead fell off and crashed through its wings. The Grand was never repaired, but Sikorsky was soon testing the even bigger Il'ya Muromets. His large biplanes served as bomber aircraft during World War I.

"What railways have done for nations, airways will do for the world."

CLAUDE GRAHAME-WHITE, EARLY AVIATOR

SPECIFICATION

POWERPLANT 4 × 100-hp 4-cylinder Argus engines

WINGSPAN 28m (91ft 10in)

LENGTH 21.2m (69ft 6in)

GROSS WEIGHT 4,200kg (9,240lb)

MAXIMUM SPEED 90km/h (56mph)

ENDURANCE 2hr

ACCOMMODATION 1 pilot, 1 co-pilot, 7 passengers

FIRST FLIGHT 10 May 1913

LEE-RICHARDS ANNULAR MONOPLANE

Although never mainstream, the notion of making an aeroplane with a circular wing has merit and has intermittently attracted serious flight innovators. British experimenters, Cedric Lee and George Tilghman Richards, designed their first powered annular-winged aeroplane in 1913.

The aircraft was built amid great secrecy at Shoreham Aerodrome in Sussex, by Gordon England. Based on two concentric steel-tube hoops, the wing was braced to pylons above and below the fuselage. At the wing's trailing edge, hinged surfaces served as elevators when operated in unison, providing lateral control when used differentially. The engine, completely enclosed in the fuselage, had an extension shaft to the propeller.

During its maiden flight the aircraft stalled and was wrecked in the resulting crash. Undeterred, Lee and Richards produced a second annular monoplane in February–March 1914. Sporting biplane elevators, it proved "delightful" to fly, despite displaying a tendency to yaw, but crashed on 26 April. A third machine was built and flown successfully up to World War I. Lee then tried to fly it himself and plunged into a river, bringing the story to a watery end.

> "The air up there in the clouds is very pure and fine, bracing and delicious. And why shouldn't it be? – it is the same the angels breathe."

MARK TWAIN, AMERICAN AUTHOR, WRITING IN *ROUGHING IT*

SPECIFICATION

POWERPLANT 1x 80-hp 7-cylinder Gnome rotary engine

WINGSPAN 6.7m (22ft)

WING AREA 26sq m (280 sq ft)

LENGTH 7.1m (23ft 6in)

GROSS WEIGHT 762kg (1,680lb)

MAXIMUM SPEED 133–137km/h (83–85mph)

ACCOMMODATION 1 pilot, 1 passenger

FIRST FLIGHT 23 November 1913

THE PILOT OF THE LEE-RICHARDS ANNULAR MONPLANE SAT IN THE REARMOST OF THE TWO COCKPITS; A PASSENGER SAT IN FRONT

THE D.5, WHICH WAS BUILT BY SHORT BROTHERS, WAS DUNNE'S FIRST TRULY PRACTICAL AIRCRAFT

DUNNE TAILLESS AEROPLANE

In the early years of the 20th century British army officer Lieutenant John William Dunne developed a theoretical interest in aircraft stability, which led him to design the first practical tailless aeroplane.

His machines achieved stability through the shaping of their wings. These were sharply swept back and incorporated "washout" – a change, from root to tip, of the angle at which the wings met the airflow. After experimenting with gliders, Dunne produced his first powered tailless machine, the D.4 biplane, in 1908, while working at the army's Balloon Factory at Farnborough.

When the War Office withdrew its support, Dunne continued under the aegis of the Blair Atholl Syndicate, set up with friends. His next machine, the D.5 of 1910, was his first practical aircraft and flew well until wrecked in 1911. Its remains were incorporated in the D.8. With ailerons on all four wingtips, this proved to be Dunne's most successful machine, flying from England to France in 1913.

Dunne had always pursued the goal of total stability in flight. His achievement in this was memorably demonstrated by a French pilot who walked out on the wing of the D.8, leaving the aeroplane to fly itself.

"The conquest of the air…is a technical triumph …so amazing that it overshadows in importance every feat that the inventor has accomplished."

WALDEMAR KAEMPFFERT, OF *SCIENTIFIC AMERICAN*, 1910

SPECIFICATION

POWERPLANT (D.5) 1 × 60-hp 4-cylinder green engine

WINGSPAN 14m (46ft)

WING AREA 48.9sq m (527sq ft)

LENGTH 6.2m (20ft 4in)

GROSS WEIGHT 703kg (1,550lb)

TOP SPEED 72km/h (45mph)

ACCOMMODATION 2 crew

FIRST FLIGHT 11 March 1910

SOPWITH TABLOID

First built in 1913 when all speed records were held by monoplanes, the Sopwith Aviation Company's triumphant Tabloid racer proved that a biplane could be fast as well as robust. Originally a two-seat landplane powered by an 80-hp Gnome engine, the Tabloid's performance proved so promising that Tom Sopwith decided to enter it for the 1914 Schneider Trophy seaplane race.

However, the necessary adaptations did not go smoothly. An initial seaplane version with a central float and stabilizing wingtip floats sank while taxiing out to commence test flights. Back in the factory, a new twin-float undercarriage was devised by cutting the central float in half; the wingtip floats were removed and a small tail float added. Fitted with a 100-hp Gnome engine, the aircraft proved itself a most successful seaplane racer. Piloted by Howard Pixton, it claimed Britain's first Schneider Trophy victory at Monaco on 20 April, averaging 86.78mph over 28 laps. Pixton then set a new world seaplane speed record of 86.6mph over 186 miles.

Landplane and seaplane versions of the Tabloid served with both the Royal Flying Corps and the Royal Naval Air Service early in World War I as single-seat "scouts".

"Aeronautics was neither an industry nor a science. It was a miracle."

IGOR SIKORSKY, AVIATION PIONEER

SPECIFICATION

POWERPLANT 1 x 100-hp 9-cylinder Gnome Monosoupape rotary engine

WINGSPAN 7.7m (25ft 6in)

WING AREA 22.2sq m (240sq ft)

LENGTH 6m (20ft)

GROSS WEIGHT 650kg (1,433lb)

MAXIMUM SPEED 148km/h (92mph)

ACCOMMODATION 1 pilot

FIRST FLIGHT (SEAPLANE) 7 April 1914

THE TABLOID WAS NAMED AFTER A POPULAR COMPACT FIRST-AID KIT OF ITS TIME. IT PROVED TO BE AN EXCELLENT RACER

WITH ITS DISTINCTIVE, COMMA-SHAPED RUDDER, THE AVRO 504 WAS THE AEROPLANE IN WHICH MANY EARLY PILOTS LEARNED TO FLY

AVRO 504

Safe and easy to handle, the modest but much-loved Avro 504 was the machine in which many thousands of pilots learned to fly in the wire-and-fabric era. Developed from the smaller Avro 500, the 504 was a pleasantly proportioned two-seat biplane, initially with a square cowling around its 80-hp engine. It had a distinctive comma-shaped rudder and an ingeniously simple undercarriage with a long "toothpick" central skid.

When the aircraft made its debut in July 1913, British pioneer, Alliott Verdon Roe, was still struggling to establish his Avro aircraft company. The 504 changed his fortunes for the better. It quickly gained popularity and over 10,000 were eventually built, using a number of different engines.

Both the Royal Flying Corps and the Royal Naval Air Service sent the 504 into action in the early stages of World War I. Its roles included reconnaissance and bombing – three 504s memorably damaged the Zeppelin works at Friedrichshafen in a daring raid on 21 November 1914. However, the aircraft was soon recognized as being more suitable as a military trainer.

After the war many 504Ks were turned to civilian use. Countless members of the public had their first experience of flight in the type, taken up for joy rides by itinerant pleasure-flight operators.

In its later 504N version the aircraft continued to serve as a military trainer into the mid-1930s.

SPECIFICATION

POWERPLANT (504K)1 × 100-hp Le Rhone rotary engine

WINGSPAN 10.9m (36ft)

WING AREA 30.6sq m (330sq ft)

LENGTH 8.9m (29ft 5in)

GROSS WEIGHT 830kg (1,829lb)

CRUISING SPEED 120km/h (75mph)

RANGE 402km (250 miles)

ACCOMMODATION 2 crew

FIRST FLIGHT July 1913

"The aeroplane is an invention of the devil and will never play any part in such a serious business as the defence of the nation, my boy!"

SIR SAM HUGHES, CANADIAN MINISTER OF MILITIA & DEFENCE, SPEAKING TO J.A.D. McCURDY, 1914

Although some attention had been given to the military potential of "flying machines", and a few large craft had been built, World War I created a need for rugged, reliable aeroplanes with engines that could withstand arduous battlefront duty. Such aeroplanes were given important supporting roles for the troops on the ground, such as aerial reconnaissance, bombing, and liaison. The need to protect aircraft performing these duties, or conversely to prevent them from being carried out, led to the development of the "scout" or fighter, and thus air combat was born. Bombers grew in size, conveying the war to cities and towns and inspiring the creation of home-defence forces and nightfighters. The operation of aeroplanes from ships became routine, the mighty aircraft carrier was born, and the flying boat became a useful anti-submarine weapon. Associated technologies, such as engines and armament, developed apace as the combatant nations vied for supremacy in the skies.

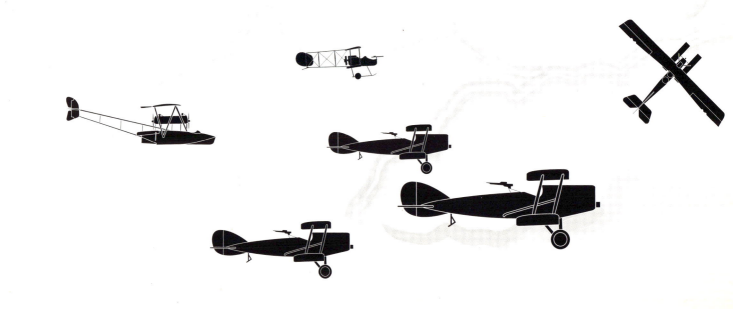

2

FIGHTING IN THE
AIR IS NOT SPORT

VICKERS GUNBUS

While it did not remotely resemble the modern idea of a fighter aircraft, the Vickers F.B.5 Gunbus (F.B. stood for Fighting Biplane) was nevertheless one of the first machines to be purpose-built for air-to-air combat. Initially ordered by the British Admiralty, the biplane eventually served with both the Royal Flying Corps and the Royal Naval Air Service.

Vickers needed to find a way of mounting a forward-firing machine gun that avoided shooting off the aeroplane's all-important propeller. Happily, they resolved this tricky conundrum by electing to use a pusher configuration. With the propeller safely tucked behind the wings, the gunner, seated in front of the pilot in the nacelle, had a satisfactorily clear field of fire.

Armed with a single Lewis gun, the Vickers F.B.5 actually went into production before war broke out. It began arriving at the Front in February 1915, and the first Gunbus squadron was formed the following July.

Although neither quick nor agile, the F.B.5 initially proved reasonably successful against German reconnaissance aircraft. By the end of 1915, however, the rapid progress of military aviation had rendered it obsolete. The Gunbus was duly withdrawn from front-line units in mid-1916.

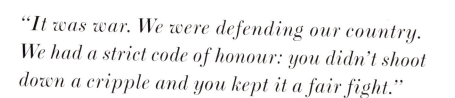

"It was war. We were defending our country. We had a strict code of honour: you didn't shoot down a cripple and you kept it a fair fight."

CAPTAIN WILFRID REID "WOP" MAY, ROYAL FLYING CORPS, WW1

SPECIFICATION

POWERPLANT 1 × 100-hp 9-cylinder Gnome Monosoupape rotary engine

WINGSPAN 11.13m (36ft 6in)

WING AREA 35.5sq m (382sq ft)

LENGTH 8.3m (27ft 2in)

GROSS WEIGHT 930kg (2,050lb)

MAXIMUM SPEED 113km/h (70mph)

ENDURANCE 4½hr

ACCOMMODATION 2 crew

FIRST FLIGHT circa July 1914

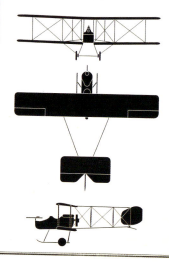

THE PROPELLER OF THE VICKERS F.B.5 WAS SET BEHIND THE WINGS TO ALLOW THE GUNNER, SEATED IN FRONT, A CLEAR FIELD OF FIRE

ALTHOUGH TRICKY TO FLY, THE FOKKER E.III WAS FEARED BY THE OCCUPANTS OF ALLIED RECONNAISSANCE AIRCRAFT

FOKKER E.III

Germany's Fokker monoplanes dominated the skies over the Western Front from July 1915 to early 1916. The key to their success was a synchronization mechanism that allowed the pilot to fire a machine gun through the propeller arc.

The first "point-and-shoot" aeroplane was French – a Morane monoplane with crude bullet deflectors on its propeller blades. It was only after examining a captured Morane that the German Army asked Dutch designer Anthony Fokker to devise something similar. As his staff was already working on a proper synchronization gear, Fokker produced the required device in short order and fitted it to his latest aircraft, the M5. The resulting E.I

("E" for "Eindecker") was quickly followed by the 100-hp E.II and E.III, and finally by the less successful 160-hp E.IV.

All the Eindeckers were wickedly tricky to fly. They could stand up to the strain of a dive, their standard mode of attack – but a pilot undertook elaborate manoeuvres at his peril. Yet in the hands of German "aces" such as Max Immelmann and Oswald Boelcke, they savaged Allied reconnaissance machines, which became known, somewhat bitterly, as "Fokker fodder".

By the summer of 1916, however, these relatively low-performance monoplanes were being outclassed by the Allies' new Airco D.H.2 and Nieuport scouts.

"Always keep your eye on your opponent, and never let yourself be deceived by ruses."

HAUPTMANN OSWALD BOELCKE, GERMANY'S FIRST "ACE" PILOT

SPECIFICATION

POWERPLANT 1 × 100-hp 9-cylinder Oberursel rotary engine

WINGSPAN 10m (32ft 11in)

WING AREA 16sq m (172¼sq ft)

LENGTH 7.3m (24ft)

GROSS WEIGHT 604kg (1,332lb)

AVERAGE SPEED 139km/h (86½mph)

ACCOMMODATION 1 crew

FIRST FLIGHT (M5) early 1914

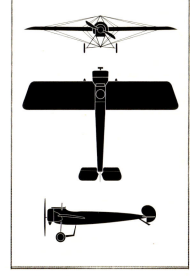

SHORT 184

The Short 184 was one of the major seaplane types of World War I. It was designed in response to a British Admiralty specification, issued in September 1914, for a torpedo-carrying seaplane with a 225-hp Sunbeam engine.

The resulting aircraft, produced by the Short Brothers' company, was designated Admiralty Type 184, after the serial number allocated to the first prototype.

From the spring of 1915 more than 900 Short 184s were built. They mostly operated off seaplane carriers, the forerunners of aircraft carriers. The seaplane was lowered over the side of the carrier by crane and took off from the water; at the end of its mission, lady luck permitting, it landed near the ship and was lifted back on board.

On 12 August 1915 a 184 carried aboard *HMS Ben-My-Chree* became the first aircraft to sink a ship at sea using a torpedo. The seaplane was also used for bombing ports and shore installations, and for reconnaissance: indeed, on 31 May 1916 a 184 from *HMS Engadine* supplied valuable information about enemy ships preparing for the Battle of Jutland. Short 184s served in virtually every maritime theatre of the war, from the Arctic to the Indian Ocean. They were still in production when hostilities ended.

SPECIFICATION

POWERPLANT 1 × 260-hp Sunbeam engine manufacturer Vickers

WINGSPAN 19.4m (63ft 6in)

WING AREA 63.9sq m (688sq ft)

LENGTH 12.4m (40ft 7½in)

GROSS WEIGHT 2,433kg (5,363lb)

CRUISING SPEED 142km/h (88mph)

ENDURANCE 2¾hr

ACCOMMODATION 2 crew

FIRST FLIGHT Spring 1915

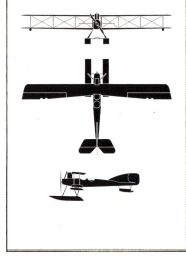

"Men were going to die in the air as they had for centuries on the ground and on the seas, by killing each other. The conquest of the air was truly accomplished."

RENÉ CHAMBE, AVIATOR AND AUTHOR, WRITING IN *AU TEMPS DES CARABINES*

THE SHORT 184 OPERATED MOSTLY OFF SEAPLANE CARRIERS; IT WAS LOWERED INTO THE WATER BEFORE TAKE-OFF

THE FRIEDRICHSHAFEN G.III WAS ONE OF GERMANY'S PRINCIPAL LARGE, LONG-RANGE STRATEGIC BOMBERS

FRIEDRICHSHAFEN G.III

From the beginning of hostilities the German Army was keen to deploy large-sized, long-range aeroplanes as strategic bombers. Flugzeugbau Friedrichshafen was one of several German aircraft manufacturers that struggled to supply a suitable *Grossflugzeug* (large aeroplane).

Their first aircraft, the G.I of 1914, failed to go into production. Its successor, the G.II of 1916, entered service in limited numbers, but was not entirely suitable since it could carry only a modest 330lb bomb load. The larger G.III appeared early in 1917.

Powered by two water-cooled Mercedes engines driving pusher propellers, the G.III could carry a 1,100lb bomb load – 220lb internally and the remainder on underfuselage racks. It was armed with defensive guns in the front and rear cockpits, but to increase its chances of survival it was chiefly employed on night-time raids.

In service from mid-1917 until the end of the war, G.IIIs were mostly used to attack French and Belgian targets on the Western Front; some, however, joined their Gotha counterparts in bombing raids on Paris and London, while others served in Macedonia.

In early 1918 the G.IIIa appeared, with a biplane tail and twin fins and rudders. The Daimler and Hanseatische companies shared production of the G.III and G.IIIa, building a total of 338.

"The aeroplane has made war so terrible that I do not believe any country will again care to start a war."

ORVILLE WRIGHT, AVIATION PIONEER

SPECIFICATION

POWERPLANT 2 × 260-hp 6-cylinder Mercedes D.IVa water-cooled engines

WINGSPAN 23.7m (77ft 11in)

WING AREA 95sq m (1,023sq ft)

LENGTH 12.6m (42ft 2in)

GROSS WEIGHT 3,940kg (8,686lb)

MAXIMUM SPEED 140km/h (88mph)

ENDURANCE 5hr

ACCOMMODATION 3 crew

FIRST FLIGHT Circa early 1917

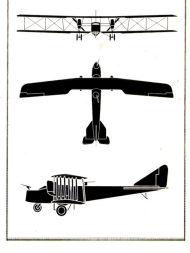

AIRCO D.H.2

The D.H.2 was a compact, little fighting scout that served Britain's Royal Flying Corps (RFC) well in the fierce air battles over the Somme in 1916. Designed by Geoffrey de Havilland of the Aircraft Manufacturing Company (Airco), it was developed from the larger D.H.1.

A pusher propeller was set behind the wings, leaving a free field of fire for the Lewis gun mounted in front of the pilot's nacelle. However, simultaneously controlling the aircraft and aiming the mobile gun was far from easy, and some D.H.2 pilots preferred to fix the Lewis to fire straight ahead, aiming the aircraft at its target.

The D.H.2 began arriving at RFC squadrons in France in February 1916. Although the aircraft's performance and handling qualities left something to be desired, it outclassed the German Fokker Eindecker.

Ordered to take the offensive at all times, D.H.2 pilots claimed numerous victories over enemy aircraft. Major Lionel Rees, for example, won a Victoria Cross for attacking ten German bombers and putting them to flight, despite being wounded.

However, the advent of the German Albatros D series soon made the D.H.2 hopelessly vulnerable. By June 1917 the aircraft had been withdrawn from the Western Front.

"…the de Havilland machine has unquestionably proved itself superior to the Fokker in speed, manoeuvrability, climbing, and general fighting efficiency."

SIR HENRY RAWLINSON, BRITISH ARMY, 1916

SPECIFICATION

POWERPLANT 1 × 100-hp 9-cylinder Gnome Monosoupape rotary engine

WINGSPAN 8.6m (28ft 3in)

WING AREA 23.1sq m (249sq ft)

LENGTH 7.7m (25ft 2½in)

GROSS WEIGHT 654kg (1,441lb)

MAXIMUM SPEED 150km/h (93mph)

ENDURANCE 2¾hr

ACCOMMODATION 1 crew

FIRST FLIGHT 1 June 1915

D.H.2 PILOTS FOUND IT DIFFICULT TO CONTROL THE AEROPLANE AND FIRE THE LEWIS GUN AT THE SAME TIME

World War I placed the aircraft companies on a firm footing: this photograph, taken in 1918, shows Sopwith Snipe and Salamander single-seat fighters being mass-produced in the company's factory at Kingston-on-Thames, Surrey.

A HIGHLY SUCCESSFUL FRENCH FIGHTER, THE NIEUPORT 17 HAD A DISTINCTIVE LARGE UPPER WING AND A SMALL LOWER WING

NIEUPORT 17

The elegant and agile Nieuport single-seaters were the premier French fighters over the Western Front in 1915–16. The Type 17, the most famous of the breed, equipped renowned fighter squadrons such as the American expatriate Escadrille Lafayette squadron, and was the mount of many famous air "aces", including Britain's Albert Ball and France's Georges Guynemer.

The Nieuports' most distinctive feature was the "sesquiplane" configuration, comprising a large top wing and small bottom wing. This was originally conceived by Nieuport's pre-war designer, Swiss engineer Franz Schneider, as the best compromise between a monoplane and a biplane. The first machine to embody the concept was the Type 10 Nieuport of 1915, designed by Gustave Delage.

Its direct descendant, the larger, stronger Type 17, entered service in May 1916. Usually armed with a Vickers or Lewis gun on the upper wing, it outclassed the German fighters in speed, manoeuvrability, and rate of climb. At some time in 1916 the Nie.17.C 1, to give its official designation, either partly or wholly equipped all the French fighter units. Nieuport 17s were also favoured by many British and Belgian pilots.

"[Flying] was extremely beautiful. On one occasion we flew round a balloon which was over Ypres and we both waved to the balloonatic who answered in a like manner."

OWEN LEWIS, AUSTRALIAN AIR FORCE, WWI

SPECIFICATION

POWERPLANT 1 x 110-hp 9-cylinder Le Rhone rotary engine

WINGSPAN 8.2m (26ft 9in)

WING AREA 14.7sq m (158¾sq ft)

LENGTH 5.8m (19ft)

GROSS WEIGHT 560kg (1,232lb)

CRUISING SPEED 165km/h (103mph)

ENDURANCE 1¾hr

ACCOMMODATION 1crew

FIRST FLIGHT 1916

SOPWITH PUP

A well-proportioned single-seater with delightful handling qualities, the Sopwith Pup was a "pilot's aeroplane", loved and remembered with fondness by all who flew it. Formally called the Sopwith Scout by the Royal Flying Corps and the Type 9901 by the Royal Naval Air Service, the Pup acquired its familiar name because it gave the appearance of being a diminutive offspring of Sopwith's larger two-seat 1½ Strutter.

The Pup entered service on the Western Front in the summer of 1916, proving a useful match for its German counterparts in aerial dogfights. Normally armed with a single forward-firing Vickers machine gun, it performed well at high altitude and showed tremendous manoeuvrability, turning on a proverbial sixpence.

As well as serving on the Western Front, Pups were operated from warships and pioneered various aspects of aircraft carrier operations. Indeed, on 2 August 1917 a Pup made the first aeroplane landing on the flight deck of a moving ship.

The Pup also undertook home defence when Britain came under attack from German airships and bomber aircraft; it could mount eight Le Prieur unguided rocket projectiles for anti-airship operations.

From the end of 1917, when the Pup became outdated for combat in France, it mostly equipped training units.

> *"[The Pup] was a remarkably fine machine for general all-round flying. It was so extremely light and well-surfaced that, after a little practice, one could almost land it on a tennis court."*

MAJOR JAMES McCUDDEN, ROYAL FLYING CORPS

SPECIFICATION

POWERPLANT 1 x 80-hp Le Rhone rotary engine

WINGSPAN 8.1m (26ft 6in)

LENGTH 5.9m (19ft 3¾in)

GROSS WEIGHT 556kg (1,225lb)

MAXIMUM SPEED 179km/h (111mph)

ENDURANCE 3hr

ACCOMMODATION 1 crew

FIRST FLIGHT On or just after 9 February 1916

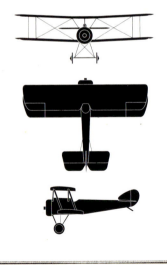

THE AGILE SOPWITH PUP PERFORMED WELL AT HIGH ALTITUDES AND WAS A FIRM FAVOURITE WITH PILOTS

CURTISS JN-4

The Curtiss JN-4 "Jenny" was the first aircraft to be mass-produced in the United States, and was described as an aerial equivalent of the Model T Ford – cheap, reliable, and ubiquitous. A two-seat primary trainer, it evolved from the Type J, designed for the Curtiss Aeroplane and Motor Corporation by British engineer B.D. Thomas in 1914. The Curtiss Type J was melded with the Type N to found the JN series.

Appearing in 1916, the JN-4 was the best of the marque. It proved stunningly successful; more than 6,400 were built in several versions. During World War I they served with British, US, and Canadian forces, giving thousands of novice pilots their initial flight training.

When war ended, military surplus Jennies flooded the market and could be picked up for a reasonable price. They were the first aeroplanes that many Americans ever saw, since they were used by the "barnstormers" who toured the United States throughout the 1920s, taking passengers for pleasure flights and performing spectacular stunts. Being slow and stable, the JN-4 made an ideal mount for wing-walkers, who contrived to clamber about on the aircraft while it was in flight.

SPECIFICATION

POWERPLANT 1 × 90-hp Curtiss OX-5 engine

WINGSPAN 13.3m (43ft 7½in)

WING AREA 32.7sq m (352sq ft)

LENGTH 8.3m (27ft 4in)

GROSS WEIGHT 966kg (2,130lb)

MAXIMUM SPEED 121km/h (75mph)

ENDURANCE 2hr 15min

ACCOMMODATION 2 crew

FIRST FLIGHT July 1916

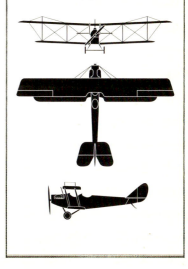

*"Great pilots are made not born...
The end result is only fashioned by steady
coaching, much practice, and experience."*

AIR VICE-MARSHAL J.E. "JOHNNIE" JOHNSON, ROYAL AIR FORCE

SPECTACULARLY SUCCESSFUL, THE JENNY SERVED AS A PRIMARY TRAINER
WITH BRITISH, AMERICAN, AND CANADIAN AIR FORCES DURING WORLD WAR I

DORNIER Rs.II

During World War I German engineer Dr Claude Dornier produced the first of the flying boats that would eventually win him fame. These giant aeroplanes reflected his abiding interest in metal as a material for aircraft construction, as well as his desire to work on a grand scale.

The Rs.I, which Dornier built at the Zeppelin-Werke Lindau on Lake Constance in 1915, was the world's largest aircraft at that time, but, unfortunately, it was wrecked before trials could begin.

His second flying boat, the Rs.II, first flew in June 1916. This was effectively a parasol monoplane, for the lower wings were mere stubs to avoid an unfortunate tendency for the lower wingtips to "dig in" to the water during a swell.

The hull was mainly metal-skinned and the tail surfaces were carried on a tubular open girder extending from its rear. The fabric-covered wing was supported by massive pairs of vee struts on each side. Initially, three engines were housed in the hull, driving the pusher propellers.

When flying tests proved unsatisfactory, the Rs.II was extensively rebuilt with four engines in tandem pairs mounted between the wing and the hull.

In tests the aircraft proved seaworthy and flew well. However, in August 1917 the Rs.II was damaged and duly scrapped.

"As the aeroplane is the most mobile weapon we possess, it is destined to become the dominant offensive arm of the future."

MAJOR GENERAL J. F. C. FULLER, BRITISH ARMY

SPECIFICATION

POWERPLANT 4 × 6-cylinder 245-hp Maybach Mb.IVa in-line engines

WINGSPAN 33.2m (108ft 11in)

WING AREA 276sq m (2,964sq ft)

LENGTH 23.9m (78ft 4in)

GROSS WEIGHT 9,158kg (20,190lb)

MAXIMUM SPEED 128km/h (79½mph)

RANGE n/a

ACCOMMODATION 8 crew

FIRST FLIGHT 30 June 1916

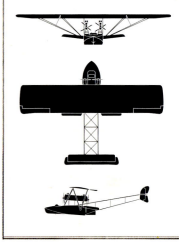

THE WINGS OF THE GIANT Rs.II FLYING BOAT WERE SUPPORTED BY MASSIVE PAIRS OF VEE STRUTS ON EACH SIDE

ONCE PILOTS LEARNED HOW TO HANDLE THE F.2B, THE TWO-SEATER FIGHTER-RECONNAISSANCE AEROPLANE PROVED FORMIDABLE

BRISTOL F.2B FIGHTER

The Bristol Fighter was one of a new generation of British aircraft deployed on the Western Front in 1917. Designed by Captain Frank Barnwell, it was a solid, versatile, two-seater fighter-reconnaissance aeroplane with excellent all-round performance. The first version, the F.2A, made its maiden flight on 9 September 1916; the faster F.2B followed shortly after.

When the Bristol Fighter first entered service with the Royal Flying Corps it was flown sedately, like a reconnaissance aeroplane. This resulted in a disastrous baptism of fire on 5 April 1917, when four out of six Bristol Fighters were shot down in an encounter with German Albatroses. Airmen soon learned to handle the machine, however, making aggressive use of the forward-firing gun, and working out formation tactics.

Used correctly, the aircraft proved a potent fighting machine. In the later stages of the war the F.2B was increasingly used as a ground-attack and bomber aircraft – it could carry up to a dozen 25lb bombs on racks beneath its fuselage and lower wing. By the end of October 1918 a total of 1,754 Bristol Fighters had been delivered. The type remained in service into the early 1930s.

"We go hell-for-leather at those snub-nosed, black crossed busses of the Hun, and they at us…Half-rolling, diving, zooming, stalling, 'split-slipping', by inches you miss collision with friend or foe. Cool, precise marksmanship is out of the question."

AUSTRALIAN FLYING CORPS PILOT, WWI

SPECIFICATION

POWERPLANT 1 × 275-hp 12-cylinder Rolls-Royce Falcon III engine

WINGSPAN 11.9m (39ft 3in)

WING AREA 37.6sq m (405sq ft)

LENGTH 7.9m (25ft 10in)

GROSS WEIGHT 1,292kg (2,848lb)

MAXIMUM SPEED 198km/h at 1,525m (123mph at 5,000ft)

ENDURANCE 3hr

ACCOMMODATION 2 crew

FIRST FLIGHT (F.2A): 9 September 1916

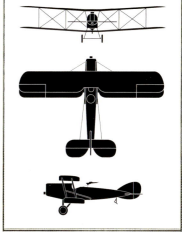

ALBATROS D.V

Entering service in May 1917, the Albatros D.V was Germany's answer to the British S.E.5 and French SPAD fighters, which were dominating the air war on the Western Front.

Broadly similar to its forebear, the Albatros D.III, the D.V had an elegantly streamlined monocoque fuselage with a cowled Mercedes water-cooled engine and a large spinner over the propeller boss. It was an excellent combat aircraft despite a disconcerting tendency to break up in a prolonged dive, owing to a design fault of the lower wing. The fighter initially equipped Manfred von Richthofen's *Jagdeschwader 1* – known as "Richthofen's Circus" because of their gaudily painted aircraft – but its performance failed to restore the balance of power in the German Air Corps' favour. In July 1917 Richthofen privately denounced the D.V as "inferior to the English in a downright ridiculous manner".

In the late autumn the improved D.Va was introduced. Externally very similar, the D.V and D.Va often served together in the same units. Both types were built in large numbers – by May 1918 more than a thousand were in service, operating in Italy and Palestine as well as on the Western Front.

"I fly close to my man, aim well, and then of course he falls down."

CAPTAIN OSWALD BOELCKE, GERMAN "ACE" PILOT, WWI

SPECIFICATION

POWERPLANT 1 x 180/200-hp Mercedes D.III 6-cylinder water-cooled engine

WINGSPAN 9m (26ft 6in)

WING AREA 20.7sq m (224sq ft)

LENGTH 7.4m (24ft 2in)

GROSS WEIGHT 915kg (2,018lb)

MAXIMUM SPEED 170km/h (106mph)

ENDURANCE 2hr

ACCOMMODATION 1 crew

FIRST FLIGHT early 1917

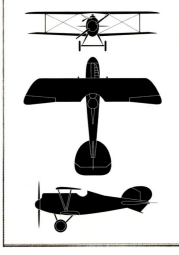

THE STREAMLINED ALBATROS D.V WAS ARMED WITH TWO SYNCHRONIZED, FORWARD-FIRING SPANDAU MACHINE GUNS

SOPWITH CAMEL

The famous Sopwith F.1 Camel destroyed more German aircraft than any other World War I fighter, although it also had an unfortunate reputation for killing its own pilots. It was named for the "hump" over the two Vickers machine guns mounted in front of the cockpit.

The aircraft was powered by a rotary engine, and engine, armament, and pilot were all concentrated at the front of the machine. This imbalance, coupled with the marked torque generated by the spinning engine, made it astoundingly manoeuvrable in the hands of a

competent flier. However, when flown by one unaccustomed to its foibles, it could be lethal.

Supremely successful in air combat, the Camel is credited with 1,294 victories between its arrival on the Western Front in mid-1917 and the end of the War.

Camels were also used for ground attack. The Royal Naval Air Service employed the 2F.1 variant, which could be launched from platforms on traditional warships as well as operating from the first aircraft carriers. A grand total of 5,490 Camels was produced.

SPECIFICATION

POWERPLANT 1 x 130-hp 9B Clerget rotary engine

WINGSPAN 8.53m (28ft)

WING AREA 21.5sq m (231sq ft)

LENGTH 5.7m (18ft 9in)

GROSS WEIGHT 659kg (1,453lb)

MAXIMUM SPEED 185km/h (115mph)

ENDURANCE 2½hr

ACCOMMODATION 1 crew

FIRST FLIGHT December 1916

"Ah, it is a Sopwith Camel. I always get confused between the sound of a Sopwith Camel, and the sound of a malodorous runt wasting everybody's time."

CAPTAIN BLACKADDER, IN THE TV SERIES, *BLACKADDER GOES FORTH*

THE CAMEL WAS A NIFTY DOGFIGHTER, BUT NOTORIOUSLY TRICKY TO FLY

ROYAL AIRCRAFT FACTORY S.E.5a

It is debatable whether the nifty S.E.5a or the Sopwith Camel was the finest British single-seat fighter of World War I. Certainly, the former was easier to fly, killing and maiming far fewer Allied pilots than the unforgiving Camel.

The S.E.5 ("S.E." for "Scout Experimental") was designed to exploit the potential of the innovatory Hispano-Suiza in-line engine; the S.E.5a, which was chosen for large-scale production, had a 200-hp powerplant. The aircraft proved to be a superbly stable firing platform for its double armament, comprising a Lewis gun on an overwing mounting and a Vickers gun on the fuselage.

The fighter was also fast and manoeuvrable, while its great structural strength enabled it to absorb terrific punishment. The first S.E 5s arrived on the Western Front in April 1917. They made tough, little adversaries for German fighters, even when the excellent Fokker D.VIIs appeared the following year. Top-ranking Allied fighter pilots such as James McCudden and "Mick" Mannock gained many of their victories on the type.

Although 5,205 were built, the S.E.5a did not remain long in service after the Armistice. In peacetime, some were converted to skywriters, scribbling smoky advertising slogans in the skies over Britain.

"After a scrap, I usually drink my tea through a straw."

DEREK ROBINSON, AUTHOR, WRITING IN *PIECE OF CAKE*

SPECIFICATION

POWERPLANT typically 1 × 200/220-hp Hispano-Suiza or 1 × 200-hp Wolseley Viper water-cooled engine

WINGSPAN 8.1m (26ft 7½in)

WING AREA 22.8sq m (246sq ft)

LENGTH 6.4m (20ft 11in)

GROSS WEIGHT 886kg (1,953lb)

MAXIMUM SPEED 195km/h at 4,572m (121mph at 15,000ft)

RANGE 2¼hr

ACCOMMODATION 1 crew

FIRST FLIGHT December 1916 (Prototype S.E.5)

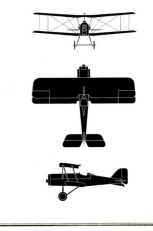

POSSIBLY THE BEST SINGLE-SEAT BRITISH FIGHTER OF THE WAR, THE S.E.5a WAS TOUGH AND AGILE

"I" STRUTS WERE ADDED TOWARDS THE Dr.1 TRIPLANE'S WINGTIPS TO PREVENT THE WINGS VIBRATING IN FLIGHT

FOKKER Dr.I TRIPLANE

A potent little fighter, the Fokker Dr.I triplane proved itself a deadly opponent of Allied scouts, especially in the hands of such master pilots as the legendary "Red Baron", Manfred von Richthofen. However, the aircraft was dogged by structural weaknesses and, in many ways, was outperformed by its contemporaries.

The Dr.I began as an attempt to replicate Britain's Sopwith Triplane. Anthony Fokker's company initially hoped to dispense with struts or wire bracing; however, the wings vibrated in flight, so a lightweight "I" strut was added towards the wingtips. The triplane was armed with a brace of Spandau machine guns on its forward fuselage.

Fighter squadrons began receiving production models in October 1917, but the Dr.1 was withdrawn after fatal crashes resulting from collapsing wings. It returned to service in late November, with the problem partially resolved.

Its capacity for rapid, tight turns made the Dr.1 an excellent "dogfight" aircraft, but it was slow and performed poorly at high altitude. Production ceased in May 1918 as the superior Fokker D.VII took over. The Dr.1 was relegated to home-defence duties.

"In a fraction of a second I was at [the Englishman's] back with my excellent machine. I gave a few bursts with my machine gun. Suddenly, I nearly yelled with joy for his propeller had stopped turning. I had shot his engine to pieces…"

MANFRED VON RICHTHOFEN, GERMAN "ACE" PILOT, WWI

SPECIFICATION

POWERPLANT 1 x Oberursel UR II 110-hp 9-cylinder rotary

WINGSPAN 7.2m (23ft 7in)

WING AREA 18.7sq m (201sq ft)

LENGTH 5.8m (18ft 11in)

GROSS WEIGHT 586kg (1,292lb)

MAXIMUM SPEED 165km/h at 4,000m (102½mph at 13,123ft)

ENDURANCE 1½hr full throttle at sea level

ACCOMMODATION 1 crew

FIRST FLIGHT on or about 25 June 1917 (V 4 triplane prototype)

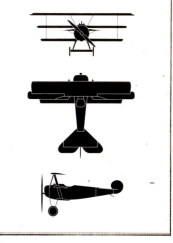

This German DFW C.V. reconnaissance aeroplane was photographed over the Western Front in about 1917. The need to protect such aircraft from attack by enemy planes, or conversely, to prevent them from carrying out their work, prompted the development of the fighter.

THE TOWERING, FOUR-WINGED P.B.31E PROVED TOO SLOW TO PROTECT BRITAIN SUCCESSFULLY AGAINST GERMAN NIGHT RAIDERS

PEMBERTON-BILLING P.B.31E NIGHTHAWK

The extraordinary four-winged P.B.31E Nighthawk proved a spectacularly futile attempt to contribute to Britain's defence against night-time raids by German airships.

The idea of a night-flying quadruplane Zeppelin-hunter was the brainchild of the eccentric British aviation pioneer Noel Pemberton Billing. It was first embodied in the short-lived P.B.29E, which appeared in early 1916. Powered by two 90-hp Austro-Daimler engines, it had a gunner's nacelle between the upper two wings and a searchlight in the nose.

The P.B.29E was followed by the rather more substantial P.B.31E. Another towering quadruplane, this was powered by two Anzani engines and accommodated its crew in an enclosed cabin. Again there was a nose-mounted searchlight, but a nose-gunner's position was provided in addition to the nacelle above the cabin. The aircraft was supposedly capable of flying for 18 hours.

The idea was that numbers of Nighthawks would ascend to altitude and patrol designated areas of the night skies until a raiding German airship was sighted, then launch an attack.

Unfortunately, the aircraft's performance was far poorer than predicted, taking an hour to climb to 10,000ft and reaching a mere 75mph. First flown in February 1917, it was scrapped in the following July.

"The heavens were the grandstands and only the gods were spectators. The stake was the world, the forfeit was the player's place at the table…It was the most dangerous of sports and the most fascinating."

ELLIOTT WHITE SPRINGS, "ACE" PILOT, US AIR SERVICE, WWI

SPECIFICATION

POWERPLANT 2 × 100-hp Anzani radial engines

WINGSPAN 18.3m (60ft)

WING AREA 89.4sq m (962sq ft)

LENGTH 111.2m (36ft 10½in)

GROSS WEIGHT 2,788kg (6,146lb)

CRUISING SPEED 121km/h (75mph)

RANGE 18hr

ACCOMMODATION 3 crew

FIRST FLIGHT February 1917

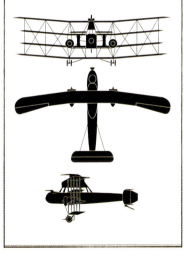

AIRCO D.H.4

Designed by Geoffrey de Havilland, the Airco D.H.4 is regarded as the best single-engine day bomber of World War I. It outpaced all but the fastest German fighters and defended itself effectively; the pilot operated a fixed forward-firing Vickers gun and there was a moveable Lewis gun on the observer's gun ring. The one major design drawback was the distance between the pilot's and observer's cockpits, making in-flight communication somewhat difficult.

The D.H.4 could carry two 230lb or four 112lb bombs. Fitted with a variety of in-line engines, it served with both the Royal Flying Corps and the Royal Naval Air Service, operating in Italy, Macedonia, Mesopotamia, Palestine, and Russia, as well as on the Western Front.

A total of 1,449 D.H.4s were built in Britain and, after the United States entered the war in April 1917, the type was adopted for mass production in that country.

Some 5,000 American D.H.4s were built, powered by Liberty engines. Nearly 2,000 of these reached the American Expeditionary Force in France before the war ended.

In the 1920s thousands of D.H.4s were flown in the United States in a variety of civilian roles. The aircraft was the mainstay of the US airmail service in its infancy.

SPECIFICATION

POWERPLANT 1 × 250-hp Rolls-Royce III (Eagle III) water-cooled vee-type

WINGSPAN 12.9m (42ft 4½in)

WING AREA 41sq m (436sq ft)

LENGTH 9.4m (30ft 8in)

GROSS WEIGHT 1,503kg (3,313lb)

MAXIMUM SPEED 188.3km/h (117mph)

ENDURANCE 3½hr

ACCOMMODATION 2 crew

FIRST FLIGHT 2 August 1916

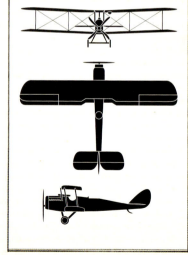

"My habit of attacking Huns dangling from their parachutes led to many arguments in the mess. Some officers…thought it was 'unsportsmanlike'… Never having been to a public school, I was unhampered by such considerations of form."

CAPTAIN JAMES IRA THOMAS "TAFFY" JONES, ROYAL FLYING CORPS

THE D.H.4's ONLY DRAWBACK WAS THE DISTANCE BETWEEN THE PILOT AND OBSERVER, MAKING COMMUNICATION PROBLEMATICAL

THE LARGE, THREE-WINGED Ca.42 BOMBER HAD LONG TWIN BOOMS ON EITHER SIDE OF THE CENTRAL NACELLE

CAPRONI Ca.42

Italian aircraft designer and manufacturer Gianni Caproni was an early advocate of strategic bombing. Hundreds of his large Ca.3 series trimotor biplane bombers were used by Italy's Corpo Aeronautico Militare in raids against Austria-Hungary from the summer of 1915. In 1917 Caproni introduced the Ca.4 series, broadly similar to the Ca.3 but with three wings instead of two and capable of carrying a heavier bomb-load.

The Ca.42 was the ultimate version of the series. The pilot and co-pilot sat in a central nacelle, with one gunner in front and two more positioned in the long twin booms carrying the tail surfaces. Two engines were mounted at the front of these booms, with a third installed as a pusher in the central nacelle. The Ca.42 carried 24 small bombs in a clumsy, albeit streamlined, gondola attached to the bottom wing.

The aircraft entered service with Italian units on 24 February 1918. The Ca.42s presented a large, easy target for anti-aircraft guns and fighters, but nonetheless carried out a number of raids. They aroused considerable interest among Italy's allies. Six Ca.42s served briefly with the British Royal Naval Air Service; the US Navy undertook to build the aircraft under licence, but this programme ultimately proved abortive.

"There's something wonderfully exciting about the quiet sing-song of an aeroplane overhead with all the guns in creation lighting out...and searchlights feeling their way across the sky like antennae."

JOHN DOS PASSOS, WRITING FROM ITALY, 1918

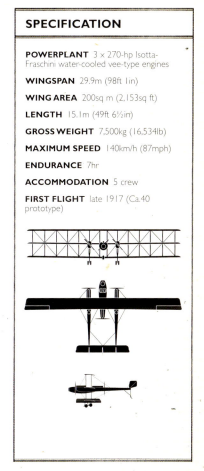

SPECIFICATION

POWERPLANT 3 × 270-hp Isotta-Fraschini water-cooled vee-type engines

WINGSPAN 29.9m (98ft 1in)

WING AREA 200sq m (2,153sq ft)

LENGTH 15.1m (49ft 6½in)

GROSS WEIGHT 7,500kg (16,534lb)

MAXIMUM SPEED 140km/h (87mph)

ENDURANCE 7hr

ACCOMMODATION 5 crew

FIRST FLIGHT late 1917 (Ca.40 prototype)

JUNKERS J.4

In 1917–18 the German Army's "stormfliers" were a potent element in warfare on the Western Front. These death-defying aircrews flew in close support of infantry, descending low over the trenches during heavy ground-fighting to attack enemy troops with strafing, fragmentation bombs, and grenades. The armoured, all-metal Junkers biplane was their favourite mount; although heavy and cumbersome, it could carry them unscathed through a storm of groundfire.

Dr Hugo Junkers specialized in all-metal aircraft construction, which he had pioneered with his J.1 and J.2 military monoplanes in 1915–16. The 1917 biplane – known to Junkers as the J.4 but confusingly given the official designation J.I – had a corrugated aluminium alloy skin that was riveted to a metal frame.

The engine and crew were enclosed in an armoured nose capsule of 5mm-chrome-nickel sheet steel, with an armoured bulkhead at its rear. To this was attached the fabric-covered rear half of the fuselage, carrying the tail surfaces. The only wooden component in the whole aircraft was its tailskid.

A total of 227 J.4s were built, production continuing up to the end of the war.

"In combat flying, fancy precision aerobatic work is really not of much use. Instead, it is the rough manoeuvre that succeeds."

COLONEL ERICH "BUBI" HARTMANN, GERMAN "ACE" PILOT, WWI

SPECIFICATION

POWERPLANT 1 × 200-hp Benz Bz.IV water-cooled in-line engine

WINGSPAN 16m (52ft 6in)

LENGTH 9.1m (29ft 10¼in)

GROSS WEIGHT 2,175kg (4,795lb)

MAXIMUM SPEED 155km/h (96mph)

RANGE 310km (193 miles)

ACCOMMODATION 2 crew

FIRST FLIGHT 28 January 1917

THE J.4's ARMAMENT CONSISTED OF TWO FORWARD-FIRING SPANDAU GUNS AND A PARABELLUM OPERATED BY THE OBSERVER

NORTH SEA F.2As WERE GIVEN STRIKING PAINT SCHEMES, TO PREVENT THEM FROM FALLING VICTIM TO SO-CALLED FRIENDLY FIRE

FELIXSTOWE F.2A

The Felixstowe F.2A was a first-rate flying boat that gave sterling service to Britain's Royal Naval Air Service on anti-submarine and maritime patrol missions.

It derived from the Curtiss H.12 "Large America" flying boats supplied to the Royal Navy in early 1917. These American aeroplanes were excellent flyers, but the hull was structurally weak. Squadron Commander John Porte of the Royal Naval Air Station at Felixstowe, Suffolk, designed a more efficient and seaworthy hull that was fitted to the H.12; the resulting new aircraft went into production as the F.2A.

Armed with four to seven machine-guns and a pair of 230lb bombs, F.2As destroyed many German submarines and airships during long patrols over the North Sea and other home waters. With some adaptation, an F.2A could carry sufficient fuel to patrol for more than nine hours; however, it suffered from a weak fuel system, often leading its crews to put down in the "drink".

Enemy seaplane fighters found that, despite its size, the flying boat was a surprisingly agile and tough opponent in air-to-air combat. In the summer of 1918, to prevent them from being mistakenly attacked by their own side, North Sea F.2As were given eye-catching "dazzle" paint schemes.

"Fighting in the air is not sport. It is scientific murder."

CAPTAIN "EDDIE" RICKENBACKER, "ACE" PILOT, US AIR SERVICE

SPECIFICATION

POWERPLANT 2 x 345-hp Rolls-Royce Eagle VIII water-cooled vee-type engines

WINGSPAN 95ft 7½in (29.2m)

WING AREA 105.3sq m (1,133sq ft)

LENGTH 14.1m (46ft 3in) ·

GROSS WEIGHT 4,980kg (10,978lb)

MAXIMUM SPEED 153.7km/h (95½mph)

ENDURANCE 6hr

ACCOMMODATION 4-6 crew, according to armament

FIRST FLIGHT Mid-1917

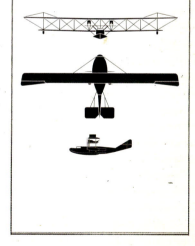

ZEPPELIN-STAAKEN R.VI

The Zeppelin-Staaken R.VI was the most successful of the German *Riesenflugzeuge* ("giant aeroplanes"). This extraordinary heavy bomber certainly justified its name; its wingspan was vast for its day and it had an impressive maximum bombload of 4,400lb.

There was nothing revolutionary about the aircraft's structure, however – like most of its humbler-sized contemporaries, it was made largely of wood and fabric.

The engines were mounted in tandem pairs, each driving one tractor and one pusher propeller. Two pilots sat, side by side, in an enclosed cabin, while other crew sat in the engine nacelles or manned guns in the nose or above and below the fuselage.

The first R.VIs were delivered to service units in June 1917, and from September they joined the smaller Gothas in night bombing raids on London. During raids in February 1918, "Giants" dropped single bombs as large as 2,200lb.

Of the 18 R.VIs that entered service, only two were destroyed by enemy fire. However, operating these massive machines at night in wartime conditions was inherently hazardous; eight were lost in crashes.

SPECIFICATION

POWERPLANT 4 x 245-hp 6-cylinder Mercedes D.IVa water-cooled engines

WINGSPAN 42.2m (138ft 5½in)

WING AREA 332sq m (3,595sq ft)

LENGTH 22.1m (72ft 6in)

GROSS WEIGHT 11,848kg (26,066lb)

MAXIMUM SPEED 135km/h (84mph)

ENDURANCE 7–10hr

ACCOMMODATION 7 crew

FIRST FLIGHT Late 1916

"The greatest contributor to the feeling of tension and fear of war arose from the power of the bombing aeroplane."

ERNEST RUTHERFORD, SCIENTIST

THE GIANT R.VI BOMBER REQUIRED TWO PILOTS, WHO SAT SIDE BY SIDE

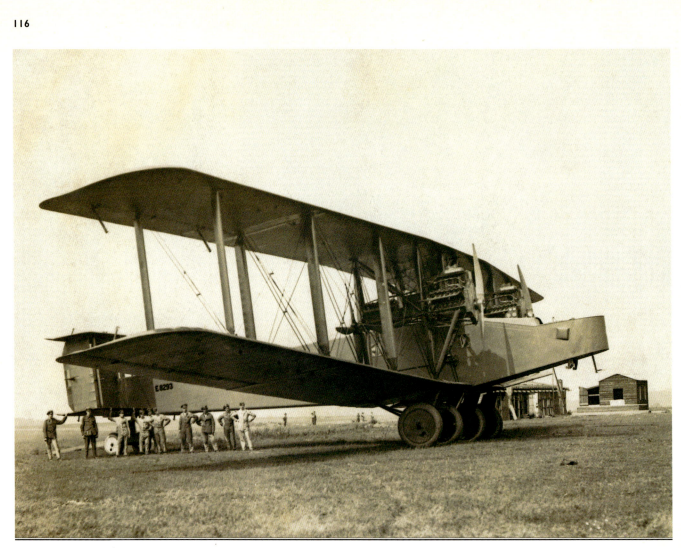

THE MASSIVE V/1500 WAS DESIGNED TO FLY FROM AIR BASES IN EAST ANGLIA ALL THE WAY TO BERLIN ON BOMBING RAIDS

HANDLEY PAGE V/1500

The V/1500 was Britain's first four-engine strategic bomber. It was built in response to an Air Ministry request for a long-range aircraft to "seriously worry Germany in centres where she felt herself perfectly safe from aerial attack". The aircraft was specifically designed to be capable of bombing Berlin from bases in East Anglia.

Handley Page responded with the largest British aeroplane produced during World War I. Powered by four Rolls-Royce Eagle engines mounted in tandem pairs, the V/1500 could carry up to 30 250lb or two massive 3,300lb bombs. The aircraft arrived just too late for war service. The first prototype flew in May 1918, but crashed; a second prototype therefore had to be built incorporating various improvements.

Orders were placed for 255 aeroplanes, but only three had been delivered by November. These were being readied for a raid on Berlin when the Armistice was announced.

The aircraft was too large, complex, and expensive to make a successful transition to commercial use. However, during December 1918 and January 1919, a V/1500 accomplished the first flight from England to India. The same aircraft was later used to bomb Kabul during the 1919 Anglo-Afghan War. Ultimately, some 36 V/1500s were built.

> *"We literally thought of and designed and flew an airplane in a space of about six to eight weeks. Now it takes approximately the same number of years."*
>
> SIR THOMAS SOPWITH, AVIATION PIONEER, ON WWI AIRCRAFT

SPECIFICATION

POWERPLANT 4 × 375-hp 8-cylinder Rolls-Royce Eagle VIII water-cooled engines

WINGSPAN 38.4m (126ft)

WING AREA 260sq m (2,800sq ft)

LENGTH 19.5m (64ft)

GROSS WEIGHT 13,600kg (30,000lb)

CRUISING SPEED 145.6km/h (90½mph)

RANGE 2,090km (1,300 miles)

ACCOMMODATION 6 crew

FIRST FLIGHT 22 May 1918

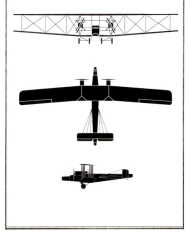

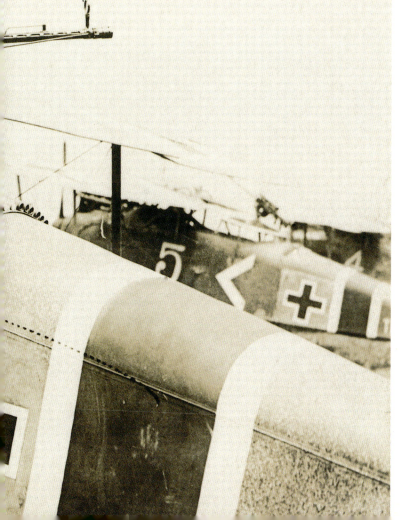

The observer of a German Halberstadt CL.II escort and ground-attack biplane checks his machine-gun before take-off in 1918. The rack on the fuselage side contains hand grenades; a belt of signal-flare cartridges is draped over the rear decking.

FOKKER D.VII

An outstanding fighter, the Fokker D.VII was greeted with relief by hard-pressed German pilots when it entered service on the Western Front in April 1918. It proved lethally effective in combat – sensitive, delightful to fly, and highly manoeuvrable.

The new biplane had been rushed into production after its prototype won a German military competition for single-seat fighting scouts in January 1918. By the autumn it had equipped over 40 *Jastas* (fighter squadrons).

The D.VII's fabric-covered fuselage had a welded steel tube frame. Its wings were wooden cantilever structures based on box spars, with plywood-covered leading edges. The system of interplane struts meant that bracing wires could be dispensed with.

Highly responsive, the D.VII could "hang on its propeller", enabling its pilot to fire the twin Spandau machine-guns when other aircraft might have stalled into a spin.

One of the many notable D.VII pilots was Hermann Göring, a war hero who later become second in command in Nazi Germany; Göring had his aeroplane custom-painted, choosing an overall white finish.

Although the D.VII initially had a Mercedes engine, later models were fitted with a BMW powerplant that radically improved its performance, especially its rate of climb. By the time of the Armistice some 760 D.VIIs had been delivered.

> *"We got into a dogfight with the new brand of Fokkers...but these Huns were just too good for us."*
>
> LIEUTENANT JOHN M. GRIDER, ROYAL FLYING CORPS, ON
> ENCOUNTERING HIS FIRST FOKKER D.VII

SPECIFICATION

POWERPLANT 1 x 185-hp BMW IIIa 6-cylinder air-cooled in-line engine

WINGSPAN 8.7m (29ft 3½in)

WING AREA 21.9sq m (236sq ft)

LENGTH 7m (23ft)

GROSS WEIGHT 880kg (1,940lb)

MAXIMUM SPEED 200km/h (124mph)

ENDURANCE 2hr (approx.)

CREW 1 crew

FIRST FLIGHT Sometime after 12 December 1917 (VII prototype)

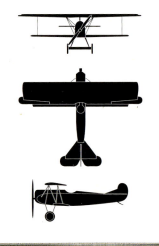

THE D.VII's INTERPLANE STRUT ARRANGEMENT MEANT THAT BRACING WIRES WERE NO LONGER NECESSARY

THE D.H.9A's PILOT'S AND OBSERVER'S COCKPITS WERE CLOSER TOGETHER THAN IN THE D.H.4, MAKING COMMUNICATION MUCH EASIER

AIRCO D.H.9A

The Airco D.H.9 was designed as an improvement upon the same company's successful day bomber, the D.H.4. In particular, the pilot's and observer's cockpits were moved closer together, improving in-flight communication between the two crew members. Unfortunately when first introduced in 1917, the D.H.9's performance proved inferior to the earlier machine. This was rectified by replacing its problematic Siddeley engine with the American Liberty 12 to create the D.H.9A.

The resulting machine entered operational service in the late summer of 1918. It saw only two months of active service before the Armistice, but by then it had proved itself to be an extremely effective day bomber.

Although only 885 "Nine-acks" had been built by the end of World War I, the aircraft went on to become a mainstay of the RAF's bomber force for more than a decade during the postwar era.

Armed with one fixed, forward-firing Vickers gun, a Lewis gun for the observer, and up to 660lb of bombs, the "Nine-ack" served against the Bolsheviks in Russia in 1919-20 and against rebels in Iraq during the 1920s. As a "colonial policeman", it is credited with saving thousands of troops from deployment to troubled British-governed territories.

> *"The air was too crowded... You would no sooner pick out someone to have a crack at, than there would be the old, familiar 'pop-pop-pop-pop' behind you..."*
>
> HARRY COBBY, "ACE" PILOT, AUSTRALIAN AIR FORCE, WWI

SPECIFICATION

POWERPLANT 1 x 400-hp Liberty 12 water-cooled vee-type engine

WINGSPAN 14m (45ft 11½in)

WING AREA 45.2sq m (487sq ft)

LENGTH 9.2m (30ft 3in)

GROSS WEIGHT 2,107kg (4,645lb)

MAXIMUM SPEED 197.9km/h (123mph)

ENDURANCE 5¼hr

ACCOMMODATION 2 crew

FIRST FLIGHT 19 April 1918 (C6122 the first "Liberty" engined 9A)

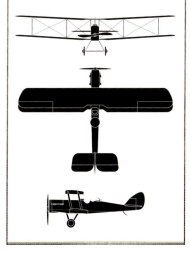

VICKERS VIMY

Designed late in World War I as a strategic bomber, the Vickers FB.27 Vimy had excellent handling and impressive lifting capacity for its size, carrying a 2,476lb bombload. It entered service with the RAF too late for active participation in the war, but was rescued from obscurity by two record-breaking long-distance flights in 1919.

On 14–15 June 1919 pilot Captain John Alcock and navigator Lieutenant Arthur Whitten Brown made the first non-stop transatlantic flight in a modified Vimy. Taking off from St John's, Newfoundland, they landed in a bog in County Galway, Ireland, after a flight lasting 16 hours and 27 minutes.

The achievement won them a prize of £10,000 from the *Daily Mail*, and knighthoods.

Then, between 12 November and 10 December, Australian brothers, Captain Ross Smith and Lieutenant Keith Smith, with two crew members, completed the first flight from Britain to Australia. Setting out in a Vimy from Hounslow, Middlesex, they flew the 11,294 miles to Darwin in 135 hours and 55 minutes' flying time, winning a £10,000 prize from the Australian government, and knighthoods. Late in the Vimy's service life, some were used to train parachutists, who were carried aloft standing on small platforms behind the outermost rear struts.

"I have lifted my plane...for perhaps a thousand flights and I have never felt her wheels glide from the Earth into the air without knowing the uncertainty and the exhilaration of first-born adventure."

BERYL MARKHAM, AVIATRIX

SPECIFICATION

POWERPLANT 2 x 360-hp Rolls-Royce Eagle VIII water-cooled vee-type engines

WINGSPAN 20.7m (68ft)

WING AREA 123.6sq m (1,330sq ft)

LENGTH 13.3m (43ft 6½in)

GROSS WEIGHT 5,670kg (12,500lb)

MAXIMUM SPEED 165.8km/h (103mph) at sea-level

RANGE Approx. 1,448km (900 miles)

ACCOMMODATION 3 crew

FIRST FLIGHT 30 November 1917

TOO LATE FOR ACTIVE PARTICIPATION IN THE WAR, THE VICKERS VIMY WAS ORIGINALLY DESIGNED AS A STRATEGIC BOMBER

STANDING JUST OVER 37FT TALL, THE TARRANT TABOR WAS STILL UNDER CONSTRUCTION WHEN THE WAR ENDED AND NEVER FLEW

TARRANT TABOR

The enormous Tabor triplane was the first and last aeroplane made by W.G. Tarrant of Byfleet, Surrey, whose normal business was building houses. Designed by Walter Barling, it was intended for British bombing raids on Berlin but it was still under construction by the time World War I ended.

The aircraft's name, meaning a type of small drum, probably alluded to its wooden monocoque fuselage. Four of its six Napier Lion engines were arranged in tandem pairs on each side of the fuselage, between the lower and centre wings; the other two were between the centre and upper wings. The centre wing had a greater span than the other two.

A 37ft 3in-high behemoth, the triplane had to be erected in the balloon shed of the Royal Aircraft Factory at Farnborough and moved in and out sideways on dollies. When it was ready to fly there was a dispute about weight distribution, and heavy ballast was put in the nose. On 26 May 1919 Captain F.G. Dunn lifted the biplane tail for take-off and opened up the top engines. The Tabor instantly turned over on its nose, killing the pilot and co-pilot and ending up with its tail in the air. A planned passenger-carrying civil version of the triplane never materialized.

"It is probable that future war will be conducted by a special class, the air force, as it was by the armoured Knights of the Middle Ages."

BRIGADIER GENERAL WILLIAM "BILLY" MITCHELL, WRITING IN *WINGED DEFENCE*

SPECIFICATION

POWERPLANT 6 x 500-hp Napier Lion 12-cylinder vee engines

WINGSPAN 40m (131ft 3in)

WING AREA 459.9sq m (4,950sq ft)

LENGTH 22.3m (73ft 2in)

GROSS WEIGHT 20,263kg (44,672lb)

MAXIMUM SPEED 165.8km/h (103mph) at sea level

RANGE Approx. 1,448km (900 miles)

ACCOMMODATION 3 crew

FIRST FLIGHT 30 November 1917

Boosted to unsustainably high levels by World War I, aeroplane production was drastically curtailed after the Armistice. Air forces were reduced to a minimum and orders were cancelled. Civil aircraft manufacturers found little demand for new products; many of the nascent airlines employed converted bombers, while private owners purchased surplus military trainers for a few pounds. However, matters gradually improved, and the 1920s and 30s blossomed into a "Golden Age" of aviation. In the wake of pioneering long-distance and survey flights, the larger airlines began casting their networks across and between continents. Meanwhile, record-breaking speed, duration, altitude, and distance flights steadily advanced aviation technology. The large flying boat, with its aura of glamour and romantic adventure, reached its zenith in the 1930s. Also during that decade, fabric-covered biplanes began making way for sleek, all-metal monoplanes with enclosed crew and passenger accommodation, retractable undercarriages, autopilots, and devices to improve slow-speed handling and safety.

3

FLYING IS A GRAND AND GLORIOUS ADVENTURE

STRONG AND STURDY, THE F13 WAS WAY AHEAD OF ITS TIME IN TERMS OF STRUCTURE AND DESIGN

JUNKERS F13

An all-metal monoplane passenger aircraft, Dr Hugo Junkers' F13 was an astonishingly advanced design for its day. Like Junkers' World War I military aeroplanes, it had a metal cantilever wing and a corrugated skin of duralumin, a strong lightweight aluminium alloy. The wing was based on a girder of nine tubular spars braced together, and its centre-section formed an integral part of the fuselage, which was built up on a series of metal frames. This structure made the aircraft exceptionally strong and rugged.

The two-man crew sat in an open cockpit, but passengers were offered the unexpected comfort of an enclosed cabin – not a luxury universally enjoyed by air travellers back in 1919. Junkers also showed an unprecedented and forward-looking concern for passengers' safety: the F13 was the first aircraft to provide seat belts.

Sales were slow to take off at first, thanks to the large number of surplus military aircraft that were flooding the commercial market after the war, but 322 F13s had been built by the time production ceased in 1932. Junkers' own transport company, Junkers-Luftverkehr, operated 60 F13s and Deutsche Lufthansa had a fleet of 55, but the aircraft also sold extremely well in export markets. Indeed, throughout the 1920s F13s pioneered air transport in many parts of the world.

"It's all right if your automobile goes wrong while you are driving. You can get out in the road and tinker with it. But if your airplane breaks down, you can't sit on a convenient cloud and tinker with that!"

KATHERINE STINSON, *AMERICAN MAGAZINE*, 1917

SPECIFICATION

POWERPLANT 1 × 310-hp Junkers L5 6-cylinder in-line engine (F13e)

WINGSPAN 17.2m (56ft 3¼in)

WING AREA 40sq m (431sq ft)

LENGTH 9.6m (31ft 6in)

GROSS WEIGHT 1,925kg (4,244lb)

CRUISING SPEED 160km/h at 2,000m (99mph at 6,560ft)

RANGE 850km (528 miles)

ACCOMMODATION 2 crew, 4 passengers

FIRST FLIGHT 18 July 1919

STAAKEN E.4/20 MONOPLANE

The E.4/20 was the first large all-metal aircraft and the true forerunner of the modern airliner. This ambitious aeroplane was masterminded by 30-year-old German engineer Dr Adolf Rohrbach, chief designer at the Zeppelin company's plant at Staaken, near Berlin. A four-engine passenger aircraft, it was initially intended for a commercial service between Friedrichshafen, Zeppelin's main site in southern Germany, and Berlin.

Astonishingly advanced, the E.4/20 embodied structural techniques way ahead of its time. Its airframe was built entirely from duralumin profiles, riveted together and covered with a thin duralumin skin. The similarly skinned high cantilever wing was based on a riveted box spar, to which the leading- and trailing-edge sections and the supports for its Maybach engines were attached. Passengers entered the aircraft through a door in the nose. The rear fuselage contained a mail compartment, toilet, a separate washroom, and luggage space. Completed on 30 September 1920, the E.4/20 made several extremely promising flights.

Sadly, however, this innovative aircraft fell foul of the Inter-Allied Control Commission, which was supervising the demilitarization of Germany under the terms of the Treaty of Versailles. The Commission ruled that the E.4/20 had the potential to be used as a warplane. In consequence, the world's first truly modern transport aircraft was consigned to the scrapheap on 21 November 1922.

"The airplane has unveiled for us the true face of the earth."

ANTOINE DE SAINT-EXUPÉRY, FRENCH AVIATOR AND AUTHOR,
WRITING IN *WIND, SAND, AND STARS*

SPECIFICATION

POWERPLANT 4 x 260-hp Maybach Mb IVa engines

WINGSPAN 31m (101ft 8in)

WING AREA 106sq m (1,141sq ft)

LENGTH 16.6m (54ft 6in)

GROSS WEIGHT 8,500kg (18,739lb)

CRUISING SPEED 211km/h (131mph)

RANGE 1,200km (746 miles)

ACCOMMODATION 3 crew, 12–18 passengers

FIRST FLIGHT 21 September 1920

REVOLUTIONARY IN DESIGN, THE E.4/20 INCORPORATED INNOVATIVE STRUCTURAL TECHNIQUES

SOMETHING OF AN UGLY DUCKLING, THE Ca.60 WAS A MASSIVE FLYING BOAT WITH NO FEWER THAN NINE WINGS

CAPRONI Ca.60 TRANSAERO

With his Ca.60 Transaero, Italian designer and manufacturer Gianni Caproni produced an over-ambitious monster to set alongside Howard Hughes's notorious "Spruce Goose". This weird, ungainly craft was inspired by the dream of aeroplanes replacing ocean liners on the world's major long-distance passenger routes.

An enormous "triple triplane" flying boat, the Ca.60 had no fewer than nine wings, arranged in banks of three. The powerplant was suitably impressive – eight Liberty engines, positioned on the front and rear sets of wings and connected by long, triangular truss-booms. Members of the crew had to crawl through these booms to attend to the engines in flight. The hull was designed to accommodate 100 passengers – a larger payload than was ever commercially carried by flying boats in their heyday in the 1930s.

Caproni's cumbersome giant was launched at Lake Maggiore in northern Italy on 21 January 1921; flotation trials began on 4 March. A brief hop showed that the Ca.60 was unstable, and ballast was loaded for the first attempt at full flight. Improbably, test pilot Semprini succeeded in taking off, but at 60ft the Transaero dipped, plummeted straight into the lake, and disintegrated. Planned repairs were never made, as what remained of the Ca.60 was destroyed by fire shortly thereafter.

"[The Ca.60 Transaero] …would not have looked out of place sailing up the English Channel with the Spanish Armada."

ITALIAN HISTORIAN, ON SEEING THE PLANE'S NINE MULTI-LAYERED WINGS

SPECIFICATION

POWERPLANT 8 × 400-hp Liberty L-12 liquid-cooled engines

WINGSPAN 30m (98ft 5in)

WING AREA 750sq m (7,962sq ft)

LENGTH 9.2m (30ft)

GROSS WEIGHT 26,000kg (55,100lb)

CRUISING SPEED 130km/h (81mph)

RANGE 660km (410 miles)

ACCOMMODATION 8 crew, 100 passengers

FIRST FLIGHT 4 March 1921

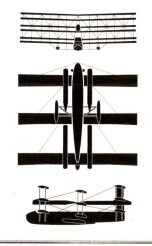

This splendid photograph shows a Royal Air Force Supermarine Southampton Mark II flying boat of the late 1920s/early 1930s. The curvaceous aircraft was designed by Reginald Mitchell, who later designed the company's famous Spitfire fighter.

POWERFUL AND SUPERBLY STREAMLINED, THE CR-3 WAS THE FASTEST SEAPLANE RACER OF ITS DAY

CURTISS CR-3

Created for the 1923 Schneider Trophy contest, the Curtiss CR-3 proved itself the fastest seaplane racer of its day. In the early 1920s American Glenn Curtiss had developed sleek landplane racers, powered by his outstanding CD-12 in-line engine. The US Navy converted two of these beauties into floatplanes, which were entered as CR-3s for the Schneider race, held that year in England, on the Solent off Cowes.

As well as having an exceptional powerplant, the aircraft was superbly streamlined, with wing-surface radiators to minimize drag. Although it was the first time that the United States had participated in the Schneider event, the US Navy pilots encountered little difficulty in beating their European opponents, who were using ungainly flying boats with large hulls.

The CR-3s took the first two places, winning the trophy for the United States at 177½mph. An admiring British observer recorded "the lean, grey form of the Curtiss racer...sliding down to the finishing line". British designer and manufacturer, Richard Fairey, was so impressed by their performance that he acquired a licence to build the Curtiss engine in Britain, a move that was to herald a revolution in British military aircraft design through the two-seat Fairey Fox bomber.

"Racing planes didn't necessarily require courage, but it did demand a certain amount of foolhardiness and a total disregard of one's own skin."

MARY HAIZLIP, PIONEER AIR RACER

SPECIFICATION

POWERPLANT 1 × 450-hp Curtiss D12 12-cylinder engine

WINGSPAN 6.9m (22ft 8in)

WING AREA 16.6sq m (168sq ft)

LENGTH 7.6m (25ft)

GROSS WEIGHT 1,246kg (2,746lb)

MAXIMUM SPEED 311km/h (193mph)

ACCOMMODATION 1 pilot

FIRST FLIGHT 1923

SAVOIA-MARCHETTI S.55

The Italian Savoia-Marchetti S.55, a wooden twin-hulled flying boat of somewhat unconventional design, earned worldwide fame through a series of record-breaking long-distance flights. Named after its designer, Alessandro Marchetti, and the Savoia company that built it, the S.55 was initially intended as a torpedo bomber for Italy's naval air force, the Regia Marina.

Its two engines were mounted back-to-back on pylons above the wing centre-section, which linked the twin hulls and incorporated the open pilots' cockpit in its leading edge. Bombs, mines, or torpedoes were suspended beneath. A gun position was fitted in the rear of each hull and the tail surfaces were carried on booms extending aft from the hulls. Some 200 military S.55Ms were built, and the S.55C commercial version appeared in 1925. But the aircraft's most prominent use was in highly publicized mass-formation flights mounted by Italy's Secretary of State for Air, General Italo Balbo.

The most spectacular of these involved Atlantic crossings. In 1930 Balbo led 12 S.55As, with 750-hp Fiat engines, on a 6,500-mile flight from Rome to Rio de Janeiro. This feat was surpassed in 1933 when no fewer than 25 S.55Xs flew from Rome to Chicago, landing on Lake Michigan. The round trip of 11,495 miles to Chicago and back was completed with the loss of only two aircraft.

"Flying was a very tangible freedom. In those days, it was beauty, adventure, discovery – the epitome of breaking into new worlds."

ANNE MORROW LINDBERGH, AVIATRIX AND WIFE OF CHARLES LINDBERGH

SPECIFICATION

POWERPLANT 2 × 880-hp Isotta-Fraschini Asso 750V engines

WINGSPAN 24m (74ft 9in)

WING AREA 93sq m (1,001sq ft)

LENGTH 16.8m (55ft)

GROSS WEIGHT 8,260kg (18,200lb)

MAXIMUM SPEED 279km/h (173mph)

RANGE 3,500km (2,175 miles)

ACCOMMODATION 5–6 crew

FIRST FLIGHT 1925

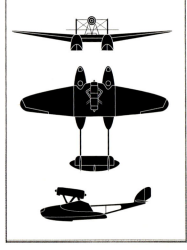

ALTHOUGH UNCONVENTIONAL IN APPEARANCE, THE S.55M BROKE 14 WORLD RECORDS IN 1926

RYAN NYP

In 1927 airmail pilot Charles Lindbergh decided to compete for a $25,000 prize offered for the first person to fly non-stop between New York and Paris. Ryan Airlines of San Diego, California, agreed to build him an aeroplane in 60 days for $6,000 ($10,580 with the engine included).

The New-York-to-Paris (NYP) aircraft was based on Ryan's M.2 high-wing monoplane, but was specially adapted to accommodate greatly increased fuel capacity. The fuselage was lengthened and the wingspan was increased by 10ft to increase lift and thereby cope with the extra weight of the fuel. The enormous main tank filled the space between the cockpit and the Wright Whirlwind engine, totally blocking the pilot's view, although a small periscope was fitted to provide the necessary forward visibility.

Contenders were queuing up for a try at the New York to Paris flight, but Lindbergh was the only pilot to propose attempting it solo in a single-engine monoplane. At 7.52am on 20 May he took off in the NYP – by then christened *Spirit of St Louis* – from Roosevelt Field, Long Island, with 450 gallons of fuel. He landed at Le Bourget, Paris, at 10.24pm on the following day after an epic 3,610-mile flight lasting 33 hours and 39 minutes. Lindbergh won the $25,000 prize and everlasting fame.

"Where am I?"

CHARLES A. LINDBERGH, UPON ARRIVAL IN PARIS IN HIS RYAN NYP

THE *SPIRIT OF ST LOUIS* FLEW ACROSS THE ATLANTIC AND EARNED ITS PLACE IN THE RECORD BOOKS

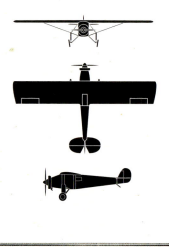

SPECIFICATION

POWERPLANT 1 × 237-hp Wright J-5C Whirlwind 9-cylinder radial engine

WINGSPAN 14m (46ft)

WING AREA 30sq m (319sq ft)

LENGTH 8.4m (27ft 8in)

GROSS WEIGHT 2,281kg (5,250lb)

MAXIMUM SPEED 200km/h (124mph) with transatlantic fuel

RANGE 7,483km (4,650 miles)

ACCOMMODATION 1

FIRST FLIGHT 28 April 1927

LOCKHEED VEGA

The stylish Lockheed Vega was a charismatic aircraft that scored high on both looks and performance. Designed by Jack Northrop for the Lockheed Aircraft Company, it was a fast, high-winged monoplane with room for six passengers.

The Vega owed its exceptionally clean lines to its smooth semi-monocoque plywood fuselage, built in two halves in a concrete mould, and its cantilever wing free of external bracing struts. The unbraced wing worried Lockheed's owner who, according to Northrop, feared that "nobody would buy the airplane unless there was something that could be seen to hold the wing up". However, the Vega proved a runaway success and 128 had been sold by the time production ceased in 1934.

As well as being used as a fast passenger-carrier by dozens of American and foreign airlines, Vegas were bought by wealth-flaunting oil tycoons and newspaper magnates. The aircraft won races and set records – American aviatrix Amelia Earhart flew one on a solo transatlantic flight in 1932 and solo across the Pacific from Hawaii to California three years later. The most famous Vega of all was probably the *Winnie Mae*, flown by one-eyed American pilot Wiley Post on a number of spectacular long-distance flights, including the first solo circumnavigation of the world in 1933.

"Ours is the commencement of a flying age, and I am happy to have popped into existence at a period so interesting."

AMELIA EARHART, AVIATRIX

SPECIFICATION

POWERPLANT 1 x 450-hp Pratt & Whitney Wasp C 9-cylinder radial engine (Vega 5B)

WINGSPAN 12.5m (41ft)

WING AREA 25.5sq m (275sq ft)

LENGTH 8.4m (27ft 6in)

GROSS WEIGHT 2,155kg (4,750lb)

CRUISING SPEED 274km/h (170mph)

RANGE 885km (550 miles)

ACCOMMODATION 1 crew, 6–8 passengers

FIRST FLIGHT 4 July 1927

STREAMLINED AND STYLISH, THE VEGA WAS THE FIRST AIRCRAFT TO MAKE A SOLO CIRCUMNAVIGATION OF THE WORLD

THE *SOUTHERN CROSS*, A FOKKER F.VIIb/3m, NOTCHED UP A NUMBER OF NOTABLE AVIATION "FIRSTS"

FOKKER F.VII/3m

In the 1920s Dutch planemaker Anthony Fokker, who had built aircraft in Germany during World War I, successfully turned to manufacturing civil aircraft in his native Netherlands. His single-engine F.VII airliner, with a Fokker trademark welded-steel-tube fuselage frame, was a huge commercial success in Europe.

In an effort to crack the nascent American market, Fokker added two extra engines to the F.VII, creating the F.VIIa/3m trimotor. It was generally accepted that American passengers would not entrust themselves to a single-engine aircraft, believing that more engines meant greater reliability. Fokker entered the prototype trimotor for the Ford Reliability Tour, a safety and endurance competition for aircraft held in the United States in the autumn of 1925. The prototype won the competition and was used the following year by American explorer Richard Byrd on a famous flight to the Arctic.

The reputation of Fokker aircraft soared, enabling the company to start building aircraft in the United States. The slightly larger F.VIIb/3m trimotor became the most widely-built interwar Fokker commercial transport, although with its wooden wing it eventually lost out to all-metal airliners. The aircraft was responsible for a number of notable aviation "firsts", including the first true trans-Pacific flight, made by Australian Charles Kingsford Smith in the F.VIIa/3m *Southern Cross* in May–June 1928.

"Motor cut. Forced landing. Hit cow. Cow died. Scared me."

DEAN SMITH, TELEGRAPH TO HIS CHIEF, QUOTED BY AMELIA EARHART IN *THE FUN OF IT* (1932)

SPECIFICATION

POWERPLANT (typical): 3 × 300-hp Wright J6 Whirlwind radial engines

WINGSPAN 21.69m (71ft 2in)

WING AREA 67.6sq m (728sq ft)

LENGTH 14.5m (47ft 7in)

GROSS WEIGHT 5,300kg (11,684lb)

CRUISING SPEED 179km/h (111mph)

RANGE 1,199km (745 miles)

ACCOMMODATION 2 crew, 8–10 passengers

FIRST FLIGHT 11 April 1924 (F.VII prototype)

Charismatic American racing pilot Colonel Roscoe Turner (in boots) poses with the Boeing 247 he flew in the 1934 MacRobertson Air Race from Britain to Australia. The photograph was taken at Heston Airport, west London, shortly before the event.

AEROBATICS BY TIGHT-KNIT FORMATIONS OF THE STYLISH HAWKER FURY DREW IN THE CROWDS AT AIR DISPLAYS

HAWKER FURY

The Hawker Fury was the epitome of the elegant and charismatic single- and two-seat military biplanes that appeared in the late 1920s and early 1930s. It made its debut in 1929 as the wooden-winged Hawker Hornet prototype single-seat fighter. On the strength of the prototype's performance, Hawker won an initial order for 21 aircraft for the RAF.

With a fabric-covered, all-metal airframe, this fighter was now named "Fury". The Fury 1 entered service with the RAF in May 1931; ultimately 118 were supplied. Hawker then developed the High Speed Fury, first flown on 3 May 1933. With streamlined wheel fairings and a Rolls-Royce Kestrel VI engine,

this entered RAF service as the Fury II in December 1936. Pilots loved it, and spectators at the annual RAF Displays at Hendon Aerodrome were enthralled by precision aerobatics performed by formations of shining silver aircraft sporting the colourful squadron markings of the era.

Although the Fury had been phased out of front-line squadrons by January 1939, having been rendered obsolete by the new low-wing monoplane fighters, 16 were still being used by flying training schools at the outbreak of World War II. Export versions of the Fury I and II were sold to Persia, Portugal, Spain, and Yugoslavia.

"Before I went into the Mess, I made the excuse to get something out of my aeroplane, and climbed into the cockpit; I did this, however, to be able to say goodbye to the old dear; and I really felt dreadfully sorry to part with her."

CHARLES RUMNEY SAMSON, WRITING IN *A FLIGHT FROM CAIRO TO CAPE TOWN AND BACK*, 1931

SPECIFICATION

POWERPLANT 1 × 525-hp Rolls-Royce Kestrel IIS 12-cylinder vee-type engine

WINGSPAN 9.1m (30ft)

WING AREA 23.4sq m (252sq ft)

LENGTH 8.1m (26ft 8in)

GROSS WEIGHT 1,583kg (3,490lbs)

MAXIMUM SPEED 333km/h (207mph)

RANGE 491km (305 miles)

ACCOMMODATION 1 crew

FIRST FLIGHT 25 March 1931 (Hornet prototype March 1929)

DORNIER Do X

When the mighty 12-engine Dornier Do X flying boat made its first test flight on 12 July 1929 it was the largest aeroplane in the world. Designed by Claude Dornier to operate on transatlantic routes, this leviathan was built on the Swiss shore of Lake Constance.

The engines were arranged as six tandem pairs on the high, strut-braced, fabric-covered wing. The two-step metal hull had three decks, and the main deck was able to accommodate 66–100 passengers in considerable luxury – the facilities included a bar, a smoking room, and a dining salon. The short upper deck contained the control room for two pilots, the captain's cabin and navigating room, and a radio cabin. The aircraft's original Siemens Jupiter air-cooled engines proved inadequate and had to be replaced by water-cooled Curtiss Conquerors. The Do X was then ready to undertake a test flight across the Atlantic.

From November 1930 to August 1931 it followed a circuitous path to New York via Lisbon and South America, encountering a number of difficulties. The return journey to Berlin the following May took only four days, but the Do X had not proved commercially viable. After a brief spell with Lufthansa the huge aircraft ended its days as an exhibit in a Berlin museum, where sadly it was destroyed by Allied bombs during World War II.

"...the joy and glory of the flier is the flight itself."

ISAK DINESEN, AUTHOR, *OUT OF AFRICA*, 1937

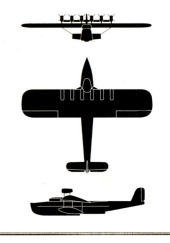

SPECIFICATION

POWERPLANT 12 × 600-hp Curtiss Conqueror 12-cylinder vee-type engines

WINGSPAN 48m (157ft 5in)

WING AREA 454sq m (4,887sq ft)

LENGTH 40m (131ft 4in)

GROSS WEIGHT 56,000kg (123,460lb)

MAXIMUM SPEED 216km/h (134mph)

RANGE 1,700km (1,055 miles)

ACCOMMODATION 10 crew, 100 passengers

FIRST FLIGHT 12 July 1929 (Bristol Jupiter engines)

A GIANT OF A PLANE, THE DORNIER Do X WAS THE LARGEST AIRCRAFT IN THE WORLD WHEN IT FIRST TOOK TO THE SKIES

Giant Junker Monoplane.

THE THICK-WINGED G 38 AIRLINER WAS THE CLOSEST JUNKERS EVER CAME TO CREATING A "FLYING WING"

JUNKERS G 38

Throughout his career German designer Hugo Junkers toyed with ideas for a "flying wing" – an aircraft without a fuselage or tail, with passengers, crew, and engines housed within the wing alone. The thick-winged four-engine G 38 airliner was the closest he came to building one.

This was in many ways a typical Junkers all-metal design, with a multi-spar wing and corrugated duralumin sheet skinning. But the wing was a maximum of 5ft 7in deep, giving space inside for passengers and crew. In addition to the 30 or more passengers in the fuselage, two or three sat in the wing-root leading edges, with a panoramic view through windows in front of them. The thick wing also made it possible for mechanics to gain internal access to the engines during flight.

The first G 38 was delivered to Deutsche Lufthansa in June 1930 and a second one followed in September 1931. At the time they were the largest landplanes in existence. The facilities offered by their spacious two-deck passenger accommodation included a buffet, a smoking cabin, two lavatories, and a washroom. No more G 38s were made, although the second prototype continued in service until it was destroyed during the war in 1941. Mitsubishi in Japan built at least six of a bomber version, the Type 92 (Ki 20).

> *"…if you happen to do any flying in early spring or late autumn, or during the winter, you will have far more peace of mind if you wear heavyweight woollen stockings."*
>
> LOWELL THOMAS, AMERICAN WRITER, *EUROPEAN SKYWAYS* (1928)

SPECIFICATION

POWERPLANT 4 x 775-hp Junkers L 88a 12-cylinder vee-type engines

WINGSPAN 44m (144ft 4¼in)

WING AREA 300sq m (3,229sq ft)

LENGTH 23.2m (76ft 1½in)

GROSS WEIGHT 24,000kg (52,910lb)

CRUISING SPEED 180km/h (112mph)

RANGE 3,500km (2,175 miles)

ACCOMMODATION 7 crew, 34 passengers

FIRST FLIGHT 6 November 1929

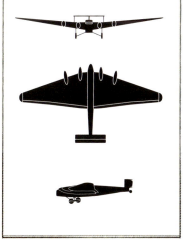

CAPRONI Ca.90

The Italian *grandissimo* six-engine Ca.90 bomber, first flown in 1929, was almost certainly the largest biplane ever built. Designed to carry a 33,000lb bombload and armed with six machine-gun positions for defence against attacking aircraft, the Ca.90 was the closest anyone came to producing the "aerial battleship" envisioned by the controversial Italian military aviation strategist Giulio Douhet. He had imagined bomber fleets attacking cities around the world, creating such terror that surrender would be the only option.

There was no doubting the aircraft's power, for on 22 February 1930 it claimed six world altitude and payload records, including a climb to 10,660ft with a 22,000lb load. The Ca.90 had an upper wing of much shorter span than the lower, a curious layout almost exclusively developed by the Caproni company. Its fabric-covered airframe was made of wood and metal. The six Isotta-Fraschini Asso engines were mounted as tandem pairs in three nacelles grouped in a triangle close to the fuselage; three of them drove massive two-bladed tractor propellers and the other three drove pushers. The bomber's paired main wheels completely dwarfed anyone who stood alongside them. The Italian air force, however, preferred smaller bombers and the Ca.90 never progressed beyond the prototype stage.

SPECIFICATION

POWERPLANT 6 × 1,000-hp Isotta-Fraschini Asso 18-cylinder liquid-cooled engines

WINGSPAN 46.6m (152ft 10in)

WING AREA 496.7sq m (5,056sq ft)

LENGTH 26.9m (88ft 4in)

GROSS WEIGHT 30,000kg (66,138lb)

MAXIMUM SPEED 210km/h (130mph)

RANGE 1,290km (802 miles)

ACCOMMODATION 7–8 crew

FIRST FLIGHT 13 October 1929

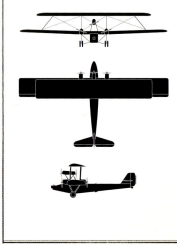

"Aviation is proof, that given the will, we have the capacity to achieve the impossible."

EDDIE RICKENBACKER, AMERICAN "ACE" PILOT, WWI, AND FOUNDER OF EASTERN AIRLINES.

THE LARGEST BIPLANE EVER BUILT, THE Ca.90 BOMBER WAS AN AERIAL BATTLESHIP THAT NEVER WENT INTO BATTLE

HANDLEY PAGE H.P.42

If any aeroplane could be described as a stately galleon of the airways, it was Handley Page's H.P.42. This extraordinary biplane was the first four-engine airliner in the world to go into regular passenger service.

First flown in 1931, it was used exclusively by Britain's Imperial Airways. The 38-passenger H.P.42W (Western) version operated to Europe from Croydon Airport in Surrey, while the 24-passenger H.P.42E (Eastern) model travelled the airline's more exotic route from Cairo to Karachi and Kisumu.

The Warren-girder system of struts between the wings permitted the elimination of bracing wires, but the aircraft's design showed a haughty disdain for streamlining. The airliner ploughed through the air at a leisurely 100mph on the power of its four uncowled Bristol Jupiter engines, providing a slow but relatively comfortable service. Eight H.P.42s were built, four of each version. They were all given classical names beginning with H – the prototype was *Hannibal*.

The H.P.42s remained in service until the outbreak of World War II, by which time they were looking distinctly antiquated among the modern monoplanes on airport aprons. But they were nonetheless outstanding in their endurance and reliability. One H.P.42, *Heracles*, flew a total of 1,318,990 miles and provided safe carriage for more than 160,000 passengers.

"Fly There The Modern Way."

IMPERIAL AIRWAYS POSTER ADVERTISING HP.42 ROUTES BETWEEN EUROPE, EGYPT, AND INDIA

SLOW AND STATELY, THE H.P.42 HAD A METAL AIRFRAME COVERED IN FABRIC, APART FROM THE FORWARD FUSELAGE

SPECIFICATION

POWERPLANT 4 x 555-hp Bristol-Jupiter XFBM 9-cylinder radial engines (H.P.42W)

WINGSPAN 39.6m (130ft)

WING AREA 227.7sq m (2,989sq ft)

LENGTH 27.4m (89ft 9in)

GROSS WEIGHT 13,381kg (29,500lb)

MAXIMUM CRUISING SPEED 169km/h (105mph)

RANGE 402km (250 miles)

ACCOMMODATION 5 crew, 18 (later 24) passengers (H.P.42E), 38 passengers (H.P.42W)

FIRST FLIGHT 17 November 1930

SUPERMARINE S.6B

In the 1920s and early 1930s seaplane racers were the fastest aircraft on the planet. Built purely for speed, entrants for the biennial Schneider Trophy contest were at the cutting edge of progress in streamlining, high-performance engines, and high-octane fuels. Britain won the trophy in 1927 and 1929 with sleek Supermarine monoplanes designed by Reginald Mitchell. For the 1931 contest, Supermarine adapted their 1929 winning design, the S.6.

Two S.6Bs were built, with a new version of the Rolls-Royce "R" racing engine and a better cooling system. A special fuel "cocktail" was created to wring the utmost power from the engine. The contest itself was a walkover,

as Britain's competitors, France and Italy, both withdrew before the event. But the S.6Bs still showed their mettle.

On 13 September 1931 Flight Lieutenant John Boothman made a fly-over of the seven-lap course averaging 340.08mph to claim the trophy, while in the second S.6B Flight Lieutenant G.H. Stainforth set a new absolute world speed record of 379.05mph. In another flight two weeks later the S.6B became the first aircraft to break the 400mph barrier, reaching 407mph. Britain was given the Schneider Trophy for perpetuity, having won the contest on three consecutive occasions. Supermarine and Mitchell went on to create the famous Spitfire fighter.

"Professional pilots are, of necessity, uncomplicated, simple men. Their thinking must remain straightforward, or they die – violently."

ERNEST K. GANN, AVIATOR AND AUTHOR, 1944

SPECIFICATION

POWERPLANT 1 × 2,350-hp Rolls-Royce "R" 12-cylinder vee-type engine

WINGSPAN 9.1m (30ft)

WING AREA 13.5sq m (145sq ft)

LENGTH 8.8m (28ft 10in)

GROSS WEIGHT 2,761kg (6,086lb)

MAXIMUM SPEED (then world record) 655.8km/h (407mph)

ACCOMMODATION 1 pilot

FIRST FLIGHT 1931

A SLEEK SEAPLANE RACER, THE S.6B USED A SPECIAL FUEL COCKTAIL AND SET A NEW WORLD SPEED RECORD

SLEEK AND BEAUTIFUL, THE MC.72 OVERCAME PERSISTENT PROBLEMS TO BECOME THE FASTEST PISTON-DRIVEN SEAPLANE

MACCHI MC.72

Designed by Mario Castoldi, the MC.72 was the fastest piston-driven seaplane ever built, although it endured many setbacks before proving itself a world-beater. Macchi built this lean and deadly racer as Italy's entry for the 1931 Schneider Trophy contest. It was powered by a supercharged Fiat AS.6 engine, comprising two lightweight 12-cylinder Fiat AS.5s combined in tandem on a common crankcase, each driving one half of a contra-rotating propeller.

This engine and propeller combination caused persistent problems. The seaplane's maiden flight in June 1931 was aborted after two minutes. Then in August, in the run-up to the Schneider Trophy, a modified MC.72 crashed, killing its pilot. Italy was forced to withdraw from the contest. Before the end of the year another of the seaplanes had exploded in the air during an attempt on the world speed record.

Undeterred, the Italians set about resolving the MC.72's powerplant problems, a prolonged effort during which they enlisted the help of British fuel expert Rod Banks. Finally, on 23 October 1933 Warrant Officer Francesco Agello, the last survivor of the experienced Macchi seaplane pilots, took the aircraft through the 438mph barrier to set a new absolute world speed record of 441mph. No piston-engined seaplane has ever been able to surpass his record.

"Air racing may not be better than your wedding night, but it's better than the second night."

MICKEY RUPP, AIR RACER AND FORMER INDIANAPOLIS 500 DRIVER

SPECIFICATION

POWERPLANT 1 × 2,800-hp (ultimately 3,000-hp) Fiat AS.6 24-cylinder vee-type engine

WINGSPAN 9.5m (31ft 1¼in)

WING AREA 15sq m (162sq ft)

LENGTH 8.3m (27ft 3½in)

GROSS WEIGHT 2,907kg (6,409lb)

MAXIMUM SPEED (world record) 709.188km/h (441mph)

ACCOMMODATION 1

FIRST FLIGHT 1931

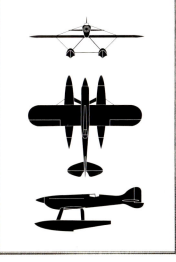

GEE BEE SUPER SPORTSTER

The ultimate 1930s American racing aircraft, the extraordinary Gee Bee R-1 and R-2 Super Sportsters were essentially engines with wings, offering a perilous but adrenaline-pumping ride to any pilot plucky enough to fly them.

Created by the Granville Brothers (hence Gee Bee) of Springfield, Massachusetts, the racers had rotund fuselages and massive Pratt & Whitney Wasp air-cooled radial engines. The cockpit was set far back, immediately in front of the negligible fin, where the designers believed the pilot had the best visibility. The two machines were very similar, but the R-1 was intended for closed-course races, while the R-2 was a cross-country racer.

Although notorious for their tricky flying qualities, the Gee Bees proved outstanding performers at American air races in 1932. On 3 September that year, during the National Air Races at Cleveland, Ohio, Jimmy Doolittle flew the R-1 to a world landplane speed record of 294.418mph. Two days later he took first place in the prestigious ten-mile, ten-lap Thompson Trophy Race, averaging an amazing 252.7mph.

Both the R-1 and R-2 were eventually destroyed in fatal crashes. In 1934 a hybrid was constructed using their remains, but this also killed its pilot, tragically crashing shortly after take-off at the start of the 1935 Bendix Trophy Race.

"My first shock came when I touched the rudder. The thing tried to bite its own tail. The next surprise I got when I landed; she stalled at 110mph."

JIMMY HAIZLIP, ON HIS FIRST FLIGHT IN THE GEE BEE

SPECIFICATION

POWERPLANT 1 × 800-hp Pratt & Whitney Wasp Senior 9-cylinder radial engine

WINGSPAN 7.6m (25ft)

WING AREA 9.3sq m (100sq ft)

LENGTH 5.4m (17ft 9in)

GROSS WEIGHT 1,395kg (3,075lb)

MAXIMUM SPEED 476.815km/h (296.287mph)

ACCOMMODATION 1 pilot

FIRST FLIGHT 13 August 1932

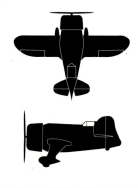

VIRTUALLY A FLYING ENGINE, THE GEE BEE WAS NOTORIOUSLY TRICKY TO FLY BUT OUTSTANDINGLY FAST

THE *TANTE JU* WAS THE LAST OF THE JUNKERS' DESIGNS TO USE THE COMPANY'S DISTINCTIVE CORRUGATED-METAL SKINNING

JUNKERS-Ju 52/3m

The most famous Junkers aeroplane – the *Tante Ju*, as it became affectionately known – was produced in greater numbers than any other European transport aircraft. Evolved from the single-engine Ju 52, the trimotor (3m) version was the last of the company's designs to employ the distinctive corrugated-metal skinning originating from World War I. It was first flown in April 1932 with three Pratt & Whitney Hornet engines, although the most common of the various powerplants used was three BMW air-cooled radial engines.

The Ju 52/3m was a supremely versatile workhorse, its various roles including airliner, freighter, troop carrier, paratroop dropper, glider tug, air ambulance, and mine-countermeasures aircraft. It operated all around the world as a civil aircraft, but from the mid-1930s it was mass-produced as a stop-gap bomber for the rapidly expanding Luftwaffe. It served in the Spanish Civil War and was ubiquitous in World War II.

Most Ju 52s were used as landplanes, but the type could also be fitted with skis or floats. The largest operator of the airliner version was Deutsche Lufthansa, which had 231 of them on its inventory by the end of World War II, most of them working on the Luftwaffe's behalf. France was a major postwar user. In total, over 4,800 Ju 52 trimotors were built.

"The air is annoyingly potted with a multitude of minor vertical disturbances which sicken the passengers and keep us captives of our seat belts."

ERNEST K. GANN, AVIATOR, DESCRIBING AIRLINE FLYING IN THE 1930s

SPECIFICATION

POWERPLANT 3 x 660-hp BMW 132A-1 9-cylinder radial engines

WINGSPAN 29.6m (95ft 11½in)

WING AREA 110.5sq m (1,190sq ft)

LENGTH 18.9m (62ft)

GROSS WEIGHT 9,200kg (20,282lb)

CRUISING SPEED 245km/h (152mph)

RANGE 915km (569 miles)

ACCOMMODATION 2–3 crew, 17 passengers or 18 fully-equipped paratroops

FIRST FLIGHT 13 October 1930 – single-engined prototype

MIGNET HM.14 FLYING FLEA

Frenchman Henri Mignet wanted everyone to have the chance to own and fly an aeroplane. Mignet claimed that anyone who could assemble a packing case could build his diminutive HM.14 *Pou du Ciel* – affectionately known as the "Sky Louse" or "Flying Flea" – and teach himself to fly it.

For a time Flea fever raged, as hundreds of amateurs started building HM.14s in their garages or backyards. The machine was a compact tandem-wing biplane. Its plywood fuselage carried the rudder, a small engine – typically a converted two-cylinder motorcycle engine – and the rearmost wing. The forward wing was supported above the pilot's cockpit by struts. There were no ailerons or elevator. Turns were made using the rudder alone, while longitudinal control was achieved by tilting the front wing.

Unfortunately, the design had an inherent flaw. If the moveable wing exceeded a certain negative angle, the aircraft could enter an irrecoverable dive. Mignet had promised that flying the Flea would prove less hazardous than driving a car, but there was soon a spate of fatal accidents and the Flea had to be grounded. A remedy was eventually found, and Mignet Fleas of impeccably safe design still fly today. But the do-it-yourself aircraft never recovered its popularity.

> "*Gosh! I am alone aboard! No messing about! A sudden feeling of anguish grips me. Very gently, I push, pull, and stir the stick. Docile and obedient, the Flying Flea responds to my orders. My mind is put at ease again.*"
>
> HENRI MIGNET, ON A TEST FLIGHT OF THE HM.14

SPECIFICATION

POWERPLANT 1 x 28-hp Carden-modified Ford motor car engine

WINGSPAN 6.7m (22ft)

WING AREA 13sq m (140sq ft)

LENGTH 3.7m (12ft 3in)

GROSS WEIGHT 250kg (551lb)

CRUISING SPEED 113km/h (70mph)

RANGE 322km (200 miles)

ACCOMMODATION 1 pilot

FIRST FLIGHT 14 July 1935 – data for the first example built in Britain

THE DIMINUTIVE FLYING FLEA WAS ORIGINALLY DESIGNED AS A DIY AIRCRAFT IN WHICH ANYONE COULD TEACH THEMSELF TO FLY

THE "LITTLE DONKEY" WAS A SINGLE-SEAT MONOPLANE FIGHTER WITH A RETRACTABLE UNDERCARRIAGE

POLIKARPOV I-16

The Soviet Union's I-16 Ishak ("Little Donkey") was the world's first single-seat, low-wing cantilever monoplane fighter with a retractable undercarriage – the formula that was to dominate the remainder of the piston-engine era. Remarkably, its designer, Nikolai Polikarpov, worked as a prisoner in Stalin's Gulag, having been denounced for "sabotage" over alleged slow progress in aircraft development. The I-16 was one of the aeroplanes that earned his rehabilitation.

First flown in 1933, the I-16 had a metal wing, a wooden monocoque fuselage, and a radial engine. One of the aircraft's advanced features, a forward-sliding cockpit canopy, was soon discarded because pilots preferred an open cockpit with a fixed windscreen. Armed with two wing-mounted 7.62mm machine-guns, later supplemented by two more in the fuselage, the I-16 fought on the Republican side in the Spanish Civil War of 1936–39. It was also supplied to the Chinese, resisting Japanese invaders from 1937.

Late in the 1930s the aircraft was adapted to take a two-stage supercharged engine, thereby creating a second-generation I-16 that entered production in 1939. At the time of the German invasion of the Soviet Union in June 1941, I-16s comprised over 65 per cent of the Soviet fighter inventory. Although obsolete, the fighter remained in frontline service until 1943.

"No guts, no glory. If you are going to shoot him down, you have to get in there and mix it up with him."

GENERAL FREDERICK C. "BOOTS" BLESSE, US AIR FORCE

SPECIFICATION

POWERPLANT 1 × 930-hp Shvetsov M-63 9-cylinder radial engine (I-16 Type 24)

WINGSPAN 9m (29ft 6¼in)

WING AREA 14.5sq m (152sq ft)

LENGTH 6.1m (20ft 1¼in)

GROSS WEIGHT 1,882kg (4,149lb)

MAXIMUM SPEED 460km/h (286mph)

RANGE 700km (435 miles)

ACCOMMODATION 1 crew

FIRST FLIGHT 31 December 1933 – TsBK-12 prototype

BOEING 247

First flown in February 1933, the Boeing 247 has sometimes been described as the first modern airliner. It was certainly a stride forward from the boxy Ford Trimotor then standard on American air routes.

Evolved from the Boeing B-9 bomber, the 247 was powered by two Pratt & Whitney Wasp air-cooled radial engines. It was sleekly streamlined, with a smoothly shaped fuselage, a complete absence of struts, drag-reducing housing for the engines, and a retractable undercarriage. Less obvious innovations included wing and tail de-icing and an autopilot. Its ten passengers were carried in considerable comfort, benefiting from sound-proofing, plush seats, and air-conditioning. A tiny galley allowed a stewardess to provide food and drinks in flight. Above all, the 247 was fast, cutting more than seven hours off the previous scheduled flight time from San Francisco to New York.

It did not achieve the dazzling commercial success Boeing might have hoped for, however, because it was initially produced exclusively for one airline, United Air Lines. Unable to buy the 247, UAL's competitor, TWA, was forced to commission its own new airliner, the Douglas DC-1, whose descendants went on to dominate the American airline market in the second half of the 1930s.

"You cannot get one nickel for commercial flying."

INGLIS M. UPPERCU, FOUNDER OF AEROMARINE WEST INDIES
AIRWAYS, 1923

SPECIFICATION

POWERPLANT 2 × 550-hp Pratt & Whitney R-1340-S1H1G Wasp 9-cylinder radial engines (Model 247D)

WINGSPAN 22.6m (74ft)

WING AREA 77.7sq m (836sq ft)

LENGTH 15.7m (51ft 7in)

GROSS WEIGHT 6,192kg (13,650lb)

CRUISING SPEED 304km/h (189mph)

RANGE 1,352km (840 miles)

ACCOMMODATION 3 crew, 10 passengers

FIRST FLIGHT 8 February 1933

PERHAPS THE FIRST TRULY MODERN AIRLINER, THE BOEING 247 WAS QUIETLY ELEGANT AND COMFORTABLE

NOT ONLY DID THE COMET LOOK SUPERB, IT WAS A RECORD-BREAKER IN THE LONGEST AIR RACE OF ALL

DE HAVILLAND D.H.88 COMET RACER

The D.H.88 Comet was a long-range racing aircraft designed specifically to win the 1934 MacRobertson race for Britain. This was the longest air race ever staged, requiring aircraft to fly 11,300 miles from Mildenhall, England, to Melbourne, Australia.

De Havilland built three Comets for the race; the first made its initial test flight only six weeks before the event. The aircraft was made of wood, with fabric skinning on the wings. Three capacious fuel tanks were fitted into the long nose ahead of the enclosed two-seater cockpit. The two engines were tuned-up versions of the standard de Havilland Gipsy Six, driving variable-pitch propellers.

The Comet looked superb and had a performance to match. When the race began on the morning of 20 October 1934, a D.H.88 piloted by Jim Mollison and Amy Johnson took the lead, reaching Karachi in less than 28 hours. But it was the scarlet-painted G-ACSS *Grosvenor House*, flown by Charles Scott and Tom Campbell Black, that won the overall speed prize, reaching Melbourne on 23 October after a journey of 70 hours and 54 minutes – seven hours ahead of its nearest rival, a Douglas DC-2. Comets went on to make other record-breaking flights, including a non-stop flight from Britain to Egypt in 11 hours and 18 minutes in August 1935.

"The Comet's nature was like [a horse]: fire crossed with passion, grace and speed. Winning a race was what it was built for and win a race it did."

ANDREW HERD, AUTHOR

SPECIFICATION

POWERPLANT 2 × 230-hp de Havilland Gipsy Six R 6-cylinder in-line engines

WINGSPAN 13.4m (44ft)

WING AREA 19.7sq m (213sq ft)

LENGTH 8.8m (29ft)

GROSS WEIGHT 2,413kg (5,320lb)

MAXIMUM SPEED 381km/h (237mph)

RANGE 4,707km (2,925 miles)

ACCOMMODATION 2 crew

FIRST FLIGHT 8 September 1934

DOUGLAS DC-3

The most famous piston-engined airliner of all time, the DC-3 was tough, versatile, and economical – a masterpiece of functional design. It was an enlarged version of Douglas's already successful DC-2, produced in response to a request from American Airlines president, C.R. Smith, for an aircraft to offer comfortable overnight travel.

By increasing the length and girth of the DC-2's fuselage, Douglas made room for 14 sleeping berths, plus a "honeymoon suite". The Douglas Sleeper Transport (DST) entered service in July 1936, but it was the conventional passenger version of the same aircraft, in which the extra space was used for more seating instead of bunks, that proved revolutionary.

The DC-3 was cheap to operate, cut journey times, and carried seven more passengers than the DC-2. It transformed airline economics, making passenger transport profitable for the first time. By 1938 the DC-3 was carrying 95 per cent of US airline traffic and serving with 30 foreign airlines. Rugged and reliable, it became one of the Allies' principal military transports in World War II, as the C-47 in the United States and as the Dakota in the RAF. When production ceased in 1947 Douglas had built 10,654 DC-3s. Thousands served for decades on civilian air routes worldwide.

SPECIFICATION

POWERPLANT 2 x 1,200-hp Pratt & Whitney R-1830-92 Twin Wasp 14-cylinder radial engines

WINGSPAN 28.9m (95ft)

WING AREA 91.7sq m (987sq ft)

LENGTH 19.5m (64ft ½in)

GROSS WEIGHT 11,431kg (25,200lb)

CRUISING SPEED 286km/h (178mph)

RANGE 1,062km (660 miles)

ACCOMMODATION 3 crew, 28–32 passengers

FIRST FLIGHT 17 December 1935

"It was the first airplane…that could make money just by hauling passengers."

C.R. SMITH, PRESIDENT OF AMERICAN AIRLINES, ON THE DC-3

THE DC-3 WAS TOUGH AND VERSATILE, A MASTERPIECE OF FUNCTIONAL DESIGN

A LIGHTWEIGHT, SLENDER FRAME AND BROAD WINGS EQUIPPED THE TYPE 138A FOR CLIMBING TO PREVIOUSLY UNATTAINED HEIGHTS

BRISTOL TYPE 138A

The Type 138A was purpose-built for record-breaking high-altitude flights, which were the object of intensive research and considerable national rivalry in the 1930s. It was commissioned by Britain's Air Ministry, which turned to the Bristol Aeroplane Company because its engines had powered many of the aircraft used in previous attempts on the world altitude record.

Designed by Frank S. Barnwell for routine flights at heights exceeding 50,000ft, the Type 138A was a lightweight, wooden monoplane with a fixed undercarriage and an enclosed cockpit. Like all aircraft intended for such work, it had wings of generous span.

Its Pegasus radial engine was equipped with two superchargers, the second of which came into operation above 35,000ft.

On 28 September 1936 Squadron Leader F.R.D. Swain, wearing a primitive pressure suit and helmet, took the Type 138A up to 49,967ft – the first time an aeroplane had flown above 49,213ft. Running short of oxygen during his descent, he broke a window in his helmet. The new altitude record lasted until May 1937, when an Italian Caproni Ca.161 biplane reached 51,362ft. In response, Flight Lieutenant M.J. Adam took off from Farnborough in a modified 138A in June and pushed the record up to 53,937ft.

"Never fly the 'A' model of anything."

ED THOMPSON, EARLY AVIATOR

SPECIFICATION

POWERPLANT 1 × 550-hp Bristol Pegasus P.E.6S radial engine

WINGSPAN 20.1m (66ft)

WING AREA 52.8sq m (568sq ft)

LENGTH 13.4m (44ft)

GROSS WEIGHT 2,409kg (5,310lb)

MAXIMUM SPEED 285km/h (177mph)

ENDURANCE 2 hours 15 minutes

ACCOMMODATION 1 crew

FIRST FLIGHT 11 May 1936

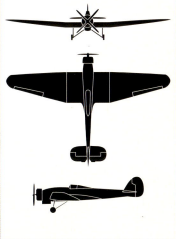

SHORT EMPIRE FLYING BOAT

Air travel was never more romantic than in the era of the large flying boats. The magnificent Short S.23s that travelled Britain's imperial routes in the late 1930s offered their privileged passengers an unforgettable experience. The principal mission, however, of the "Empire" flying boats was the transportation of mail.

It was in order to fulfil the terms of its Empire Air Mail Scheme that the British government initially ordered a fleet of 28 for Imperial Airways from Short Brothers. Known as the "C" class, because each aircraft had a name beginning with that letter, the flying boats were advanced, streamlined, all-metal monoplanes. By the standards of their day, they were impressively large and powerful, capable of carrying heavy payloads at relatively high speeds – they covered the longest of their routes, from London to Sydney, in nine days with overnight stops.

In total, 31 S.23s and 11 related types were built. Although eight were lost in fatal crashes during their first three years, the C-class flying boats remained in service for more than a decade from 1936. During World War II they flew BOAC's "Horseshoe Route" to Australia via East Africa and India, while two S.23s and two S.30s served in the Royal Air Force. Sadly, only 13 Empire flying boats survived the war, and by the end of 1947 they had all been withdrawn from service.

SPECIFICATION

POWERPLANT 4 x 910-hp Bristol Pegasus XC 9-cylinder radial engines

WINGSPAN 34.8m (114ft)

WING AREA 139.4sq m (1,500sq ft)

LENGTH 26.8m (88ft)

GROSS WEIGHT 18,371kg (40,500lb)

MAXIMUM SPEED 322km/h (200mph)

ACCOMMODATION 3–4 crew, 24 passengers

FIRST FLIGHT 4 July 1936

"Every flyer who ventures across oceans to distant lands is a potential explorer…Riding through the air on silver wings instead of sailing the sea with white wings, he must steer his own course, for the air is uncharted."

JEAN BATTEN, NEW ZEALAND AVIATRIX, WRITING IN *ALONE IN THE SKY*

THE STATELY SHORT EMPIRE FLYING BOATS MADE IMPERIAL AIRWAYS THE WORLD'S LARGEST CARRIER OF MAIL

United States Army Air Corps pilots demonstrate their formation-flying skills in their Seversky P-35A single-seat pursuit aircraft during training in April 1939. The P-35 was a forebear of the famous Republic P-47 Thunderbolt of World War II.

THE BOEING 314 GAVE WEALTHY PASSENGERS A LUXURIOUS FLIGHT ON TRANSOCEANIC ROUTES

BOEING 314

The Boeing 314 "Clipper" flying boat was probably the most luxurious passenger aeroplane ever built. This stately giant was created for Pan American, who wanted an aircraft to carry wealthy passengers in comfort and style on transoceanic routes.

Boeing married the wings and tailplane of their prototype XB-15 long-range bomber with a massive whale-shaped hull to make a flying boat of breathtaking size. The hull provided spacious accommodation for 74 seated passengers or 40 in sleeping berths. These lucky travellers benefited from a plush lounge, dressing rooms, and a dining salon where waiters served gourmet food prepared by on-board chefs.

The first six 314s were delivered in the first half of 1939. Pan American inaugurated a transatlantic mail service in May, followed in June by the first scheduled passenger service across the North Atlantic. Only three months later the onset of World War II brought the newly established service to an abrupt halt.

Pan Am bought a further six upgraded 314As in 1941, and the flying boats flew through the war in a variety of roles, including ferrying President Roosevelt and Prime Minister Churchill to top-level wartime meetings. But by the time the war ended, the progress of landplanes had made the flying boat obsolete and Pan American stopped operating 314s in 1946.

"Half boat, half aeroplane, taking off in a tumult of spray – the flying boat was a journey of a lifetime."

GRAHAM COSTNER, AUTHOR, WRITING IN *CORSAIRVILLE: THE LOST DOMAIN OF THE FLYING BOAT*

SPECIFICATION

POWERPLANT 4 × 1,600-hp Wright GR-2600-A2 "Double Cyclone" 14-cylinder radial engines

WINGSPAN 46.3m (152ft)

WING AREA 266.3sq m (2,867sq ft)

LENGTH 32.3m (106ft)

GROSS WEIGHT 37,422kg (82,500lb)

CRUISING SPEED 295km/h (183mph)

RANGE 5,633km (3,500 miles)

ACCOMMODATION 10 crew, 74 passengers

FIRST FLIGHT 7 June 1938

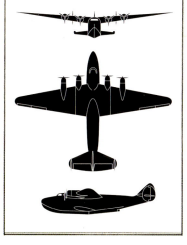

BOEING MODEL 307 STRATOLINER

The Boeing 307 Stratoliner was the world's first airliner to have a pressurized passenger cabin. This meant that it could fly in the cloudless blue of the stratosphere, high above the turbulent weather that had previously so often made flight a trying experience for passengers.

The 307 was created as a spin-off of Boeing's top military project, the development of which would become the B-17 Flying Fortress bomber. Boeing combined the bomber's wings, tail, and powerplant with an all-new, fatter fuselage. The engines had turbo-superchargers to make them efficient for cruising at high altitude, giving the aircraft a substantial speed advantage over the Douglas DC-3, which was dominant in the US airliner market at the time.

The first 307 was unfortunately destroyed during a test flight in March 1939, but in 1940 three Stratoliners were delivered to Pan American and four to TWA. In the years preceding the United States' entry into World War II, the Stratoliners were heavily used: the TWA fleet flew 4,522,500 accident-free miles. During the war they were employed as military transports, but by the time peace returned newer airliners had left the 307 far behind. One Stratoliner had been sold to millionaire Howard Hughes in 1939 for his personal use; it was later converted into a houseboat at Fort Lauderdale, Florida.

"I think it is a pity to lose the romantic side of flying and simply to accept it as a common means of transport, although that end is what we have all ostensibly been striving to attain."

AMY JOHNSON, AVIATRIX

SPECIFICATION

POWERPLANT 4 × 1,100-hp Wright GR-1820-G105A Cyclone 9-cylinder radial engines

WINGSPAN 32.7m (107ft 3in)

WING AREA 138sq m (1,486 sq ft)

LENGTH 22.7m (74ft 4in)

GROSS WEIGHT 20,412kg (45,000lb)

CRUISING SPEED 357km/h (222mph)

RANGE 2,696km (1,675 miles)

ACCOMMODATION 5 crew, 33 passengers

FIRST FLIGHT 31 December 1938

THE 307 WAS THE FIRST AIRLINER TO BE ABLE TO PROVIDE A SMOOTH FLIGHT IN THE BLUE SKIES HIGH ABOVE THE CLOUDS

World War II stimulated another divergence in the aeroplane's development. The few biplanes surviving in front-line units quickly disappeared, while many of the advances in late-1930s civil aviation were hurriedly adapted for military use. Armament had improved little in the interwar period, but heavily-armed fighters soon predominated. High-speed bombers required efficient, power-operated turrets for their defensive weaponry, and bomb capacities and range also increased. Flying boats again proved valuable for patrol and anti-submarine work. Ground-attack, a role that had evolved at the end of World War I, assumed greater significance as control of airspace over a battlefield became vital. The aircraft carrier played a prominent part in the war at sea. Following initial experiments in the 1930s, the jet engine became a practical proposition and the first jet-propelled fighters and bombers appeared towards the end of the war.

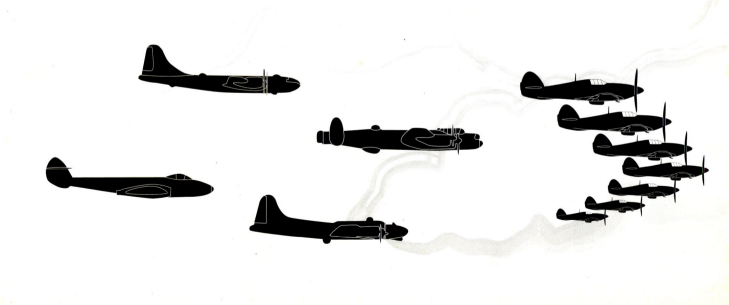

4

1939–1945

BANDITS AT TWO O'CLOCK

STURDY AND RELIABLE, THE HAWKER HURRICANE WAS ONE OF THE RAF's MOST SUCCESSFUL FIGHTERS OF WORLD WAR II

HAWKER HURRICANE

The doughty Hawker Hurricane single-seat fighter is famous for destroying more enemy aircraft than any other Allied fighter during World War II. Designed by Sydney Camm, it made its maiden flight in November 1935. When the Hurricane entered service in December 1937, it was the Royal Air Force's (RAF's) first monoplane fighter and its first aircraft with a top speed greater than 300mph. The eight-gun armament was also unprecedented. Yet, with a tubular metal frame covered in wood and fabric, it was structurally a trifle old-fashioned compared with its all-metal contemporaries.

The Hurricane was soon upstaged by the introduction of the more glamorous Spitfire, which was superior in speed and climb. But the Hurricane was easier to build and repair, and its sturdy structure could absorb substantial punishment. Although the Spitfire took the glory, it was the Hurricane that proved the mainstay of RAF Fighter Command in the Battle of Britain in 1940. No fewer than 1,715 were flown during that epic conflict, and four-fifths of the enemy aircraft destroyed fell to their guns.

Various versions of the Hurricane emerged during the course of the war, with upgraded engines and adapted to a wide variety of roles, including ground-attack and anti-tank missions. In total, more than 14,000 Hurricanes were produced.

"I threw my Hurricane around as best I could and whenever a Hun came into my sights, I pressed the button. It was truly...the most exhilarating time I have ever had in my life."

ROALD DAHL, WWII PILOT AND AUTHOR, WRITING IN *GOING SOLO*

SPECIFICATION

POWERPLANT 1 × 1,030-hp Rolls-Royce Merlin II 12-cylinder liquid-cooled vee engine (Mk I)

WINGSPAN 12.2m (40ft)

WING AREA 23.9sq m (258sq ft)

LENGTH 9.5m (31ft 4in)

GROSS WEIGHT 2,820kg (6,218lb)

MAXIMUM SPEED 518km/h at 6,096m (322mph at 20,000ft)

RANGE 845km (525 miles)

ACCOMMODATION 1 crew

FIRST FLIGHT 6 November 1935

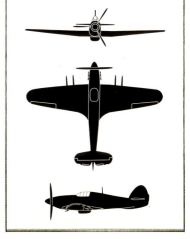

MESSERSCHMITT Bf 109

Designed by Willy Messerschmitt, the Bf 109 fighter was the great adversary of the Hurricane and Spitfire during the Battle of Britain. When it first flew, in September 1935, the lightweight Bf 109 was probably the world's most advanced fighter aircraft, made entirely of metal, with a retractable undercarriage and an enclosed cockpit.

Blooded with the Condor Legion in the Spanish Civil War, the Bf 109 proved a good gun platform, steady and fast in combat, but it took considerable strength to pull it out of a dive and had a tendency to swing to port in take-off and landing.

Combined with an unsatisfactory narrow undercarriage, this caused around one in 20 Messerschmitts to be written off in landing accidents.

The Bf 109E, the variant that fought in the Battle of Britain, had a 20mm cannon firing through its propeller spinner. Operating at the limit of its range over southern England, it proved more than a match for the RAF fighters. It was faster in a dive than the Hurricane or Spitfire and capable of impressive high-g turns. Later versions included the aerodynamically refined Bf 109F and the Bf 109G. Some 35,000 of all marks were built in total.

"The new Bf 109 simply looks fabulous. The take-off is certainly unusual but…its flight characteristics are fantastic."

JOHANNES TRAUTLOFT, CONDOR LEGION PILOT

THE REDOUBTABLE Bf 109 WAS A POTENT FIGHTER CAPABLE OF PERFORMING DAZZLING HIGH-G TURNS AND SWIFT DIVES

SPECIFICATION

POWERPLANT 1 × 1,150-hp inverted, liquid-cooled Daimler-Benz DB 601A 12-cylinder liquid-cooled engine (Bf 109E-4)

WINGSPAN 9.8m (32ft 4¼in)

WING AREA 16.4sq m (177sq ft)

LENGTH 8.6m (28ft 4in)

GROSS WEIGHT 2,505kg (5,523lb)

MAXIMUM SPEED 570km/h at 3,800m (354mph at 12,460ft)

RANGE 660km (410 miles)

ACCOMMODATION 1 crew

FIRST FLIGHT September 1935

THE Ju 87 STUKA DIVE-BOMBER HAD AN UNUSUAL "INVERTED-GULL" WING AND A FIXED UNDERCARRIAGE

JUNKERS Ju 87 STUKA

Used as "aerial artillery" to support fast-moving armoured columns, the Ju 87 "Stuka" dive-bomber played a memorable part in Germany's Blitzkrieg offensives of 1939–40. The two-seat, all-metal aircraft with its distinctive "inverted-gull" wing and fixed undercarriage first made its appearance in 1935. A handful of first-production Ju 87As were given a trial run during the Spanish Civil War, but it was during the German invasion of Poland in September 1939 and the subsequent defeat of France that the Stukas really came into their own.

Emitting a banshee wail from "Jericho trumpet" sirens fitted in their wheel spats, they attacked in a steep dive, bombing ground targets while simultaneously terrorizing soldiers and civilians alike. The Stukas were also a highly effective weapon against shipping, as they demonstrated in the terrible bludgeoning of the carrier *Illustrious* in January 1941.

The aircraft's relatively slow and cumbersome progress proved a fatal drawback, however, as it made them easy prey for high-performance fighters. It had to be withdrawn early in the Battle of Britain, following savagings by Spitfires and Hurricanes. Ju 87s continued to prove their worth in less hotly contested airspace, operating effectively on the Eastern Front well into the later stages of the war.

"Air power may either end war or end civilization."

SIR WINSTON CHURCHILL, BRITISH STATESMAN AND AUTHOR

SPECIFICATION

POWERPLANT 1 × 1,217-hp Junkers Jumo 211 Da 12-cylinder liquid-cooled engine (Ju 87B-2)

WINGSPAN 13.8m (45ft 3¼in)

WING AREA 31.9sq m (343sq ft)

LENGTH 11.1m (36ft 5in)

GROSS WEIGHT 4,390kg (9678.3lb) with a 500kg (1,102lb) bombload

MAXIMUM SPEED 326km/h at 2,000m (203mph at 6,562ft)

RANGE 595km (370 miles)

ACCOMMODATION 2 crew

FIRST FLIGHT 17 September 1935

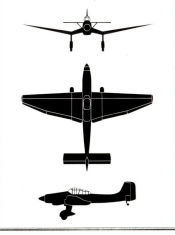

BOEING B-17 FLYING FORTRESS

During World War II the daylight raids on Germany by massed formations of B-17 bombers were a supreme expression of the US's military and industrial might. The B-17s were designed to penetrate hostile airspace without fighter escort, relying on their impressive speed, altitude, and collective firepower for survival.

They certainly earned the "Flying Fortress" tag and bristled with guns, including two in the extraordinary Sperry ball turret beneath the fuselage – a cramped position that only a small man could occupy. The bombardier sat in the Plexiglas nose, equipped with the top-secret Norden bombsight that was supposed to ensure precision bombing.

When the B-17s went into action against targets in Europe in 1943, they found shooting their way in and out much tougher than anticipated. Both German fighters and flak took a heavy toll of the bombers. The B-17 provided few creature comforts for its crew, who had to fly at altitudes of over **30,000** feet in an unpressurized, unheated aircraft, but they appreciated its ability to absorb punishment and survive.

The advent of long-range escort fighters eventually shifted the air war decisively in the bombers' favour. Yet even when losses were high, the US's factories could always manufacture far more B-17s than were ever lost in action.

"Without the B-17, we might have lost the war."

GENERAL CARL SPAATZ, COMMANDER, US STRATEGIC AIR FORCES IN EUROPE, 1944

SPECIFICATION

POWERPLANT 4 × 1,200-hp Wright R-1820-97 air-cooled radials with General Electric B-22 turbo-superchargers (B-17G)

WINGSPAN 31.6m (103ft 9in)

WING AREA 131.9sq m (1,420sq ft)

LENGTH 22.8m (74ft 4in)

GROSS WEIGHT 24,948kg (55,000lb)

MAXIMUM SPEED 486km/h at 7,620m (302mph at 25,000ft)

RANGE 3,220km (2,000 miles) with a 2,772 kg (6,000lb) bombload

ACCOMMODATION 10 crew

FIRST FLIGHT 28 July 1935

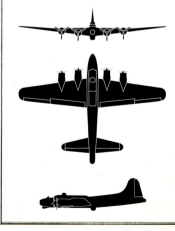

ONE OF WORLD WAR II's GREAT HEAVY BOMBERS, THE FLYING FORTRESS WAS USED FOR HIGH-ALTITUDE DAYLIGHT RAIDS

Hawker Hurricane Mk I fighters of
73 Squadron, Royal Air Force, patrol
over the Western Front in France in
the early days of World War II, as part
of the Advanced Air Striking Force.

RUGGED AND RELIABLE, THE WELLINGTON ESTABLISHED A SOLID REPUTATION AS A NIGHT-BOMBER

VICKERS WELLINGTON

The twin-engined Wellington, affectionately known as the "Wimpy", was the RAF's most advanced bomber aircraft going into World War II. It boasted a "geodetic" construction patented by inventor Barnes Wallis, its fuselage and wings being formed from a latticework of intersecting aluminium units, but could only be fabric-covered, a major disadvantage. However, the resulting airframe was light, damage-resistant, and easily repaired. This was extremely fortunate, as the slow and somewhat inadequately armed bomber often had to take a great deal of punishment.

At the beginning of the war it was used in daylight raids against German warships and ports. However, it proved hopelessly vulnerable to enemy fighters, and shocking early losses led to its transfer to night-time operations; this sharply increased its chances of survival, although the odds were stacked against it finding its target.

In April 1941 a Wellington was the first bomber to drop a 4,000lb "blockbuster" bomb on Germany. With steadily improving armament and various changes in powerplant, the Wellington soldiered on in the night-bomber role until October 1943, earning a reputation for reliability and ruggedness. The aircraft also served with Coastal Command, destroying 28 U-boats and torpedoing enemy vessels in the Mediterranean. After retirement from the front line, the Wellington was used as a bomber-crew trainer.

"It is generally inadvisable to eject directly over the area you just bombed."

US AIR FORCE MANUAL

SPECIFICATION

POWERPLANT 2 x 1,050-hp Bristol Pegasus XVIII radial engines (B Mk I)

WINGSPAN 26.3m (86ft 2in)

WING AREA 78sq m (840sq ft)

LENGTH 19.7m (64ft 7in)

GROSS WEIGHT 8,415kg (25,800lb)

MAXIMUM SPEED 378km/h (235mph)

RANGE 2,905km (1,805 miles)

ACCOMMODATION 6 crew

FIRST FLIGHT 15 June 1936

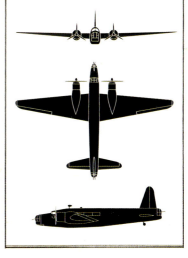

SUPERMARINE SPITFIRE

This superb fighter, designed by Reginald Mitchell, will always be remembered as the RAF's outstanding fighter of World War II, and especially for the vital part it played in the Battle of Britain. Powered by the Rolls-Royce Merlin engine, the Spitfire combined all the most advanced features of its time: a variable-pitch propeller; all-metal monocoque construction; a retractable undercarriage; and an enclosed cockpit.

Its uniqueness lay in the elliptical wing. This deftly solved the problem of housing eight machine guns and a retracted undercarriage, while providing enough strength to withstand high-stress manoeuvres. There were a few drawbacks. The novel wing construction meant that the aircraft was relatively difficult to manufacture and early versions of the engine often cut out going into a dive.

But the Spitfire was a joy for an experienced pilot to fly, responsive to the slightest touch of the controls. Its blend of sleek elegance and fighting efficiency was summed up by RAF pilot Adolf "Sailor" Malan: "The Spitfire," he said, "had style and was obviously a killer." The overall quality of the design was proved by the aircraft's ability to hold its own throughout the war in a string of different versions tailored to specialist roles and powered by progressively upgraded engines.

SPECIFICATION

POWERPLANT 1 x 1,175-hp Rolls-Royce Merlin XII 12-cylinder liquid-cooled vee-type engine (Mk IIA)

WINGSPAN 22.5sq m (242sq ft)

LENGTH 9.1m (29ft 11in)

GROSS WEIGHT 2,803kg (6,172lb)

MAXIMUM SPEED 570km/h at 5,349m (354mph at 17,554ft)

RANGE 637km (395 miles)

ACCOMMODATION 1 crew

FIRST FLIGHT 5 March 1936 (K5054 – Supermarine Type 300)

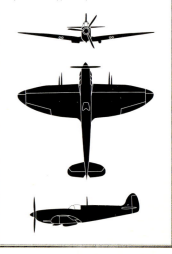

"I think every Spitfire pilot fell in love with it as soon as he sat in that nice tight cosy office [RAF slang for cockpit] with everything to hand."

BOB STANFORD-TUCK, RAF FIGHTER-PILOT, WWII

THIN WINGS, A SMALL FUSELAGE SECTION, AND REFINED STREAMLINING MADE THE SPITFIRE BOTH ELEGANT AND FAST

A LONG-RANGE RECONNAISSANCE AND ANTISUBMARINE PATROL AIRCRAFT, THE SUNDERLAND HAD UP TO 12 DEFENSIVE GUNS

SHORT SUNDERLAND

Few warplanes have been as graceful as the Short Sunderland flying boat, nor as consistently effective in performance. Evolved from the same company's stately Empire flying boats, the Sunderland entered service with RAF Coastal Command in June 1938 as a long-range reconnaissance and antisubmarine patrol aircraft.

When war broke out the following year, it became a vital element in Britain's desperate struggle to keep sea lanes open across the North Atlantic, escorting merchant convoys, and hunting down U-boats. On its long and lonely ocean patrols, the Sunderland needed to be able to defend itself unaided in any chance encounter with German aircraft.

The Germans learned to respect the flying boat's firepower and gave it the nickname "Flying Porcupine" because it bristled with up to 12 defensive guns. Many Allied soldiers and sailors owed their lives to the Sunderland, which saved the crews of torpedoed ships and carried out rescue operations during the evacuations of Norway, Greece, and Crete.

In total, 749 were built, and at the war's end there were 28 Sunderland-equipped squadrons. In the postwar period Sunderlands were used in the Berlin Airlift and the Korean War. When they were retired in 1959, the RAF finally said farewell to flying boats.

"It was no picnic despite what anyone might say later…Most of us were pretty scared all the bloody time; you only felt happy when the battle was over and you were on your way home, then you were safe for a bit, anyway."

COLIN GRAY, 54 SQUADRON RAF, WWII

SPECIFICATION

POWERPLANT 4 × 1,200-hp Pratt & Whitney R-1830-90B Twin Wasp 14-cylinder radial engines (Mk V)

WINGSPAN 34.4m (112ft 9½in)

WING AREA 156.7sq m (1,687sq ft)

LENGTH 26m (85ft 3½in)

GROSS WEIGHT 29,484kg (65,000lb)

CRUISING SPEED 214km/h at 610m (133mph at 2,000ft)

RANGE 4,329km with 757kg (2,690 miles with 1,668lb) bombload

ACCOMMODATION 13 crew

FIRST FLIGHT 16 October 1937

ILYUSHIN II-2 SHTURMOVIK

The Soviet Ilyushin Il-2 Shturmovik ground-attack aircraft was produced in greater numbers than any other aeroplane in history – at least 35,952 were made. Crudely built as an expendable item, it was not designed to be taken apart or extensively repaired. For maximum protection during ground-attack operations, the crew and engine were enclosed in a "bathtub" of heavy armour plate, to which the all-metal rear fuselage and wings were attached.

Designed by Sergei Ilyushin as a two-seater, the Il-2 entered service in single-seat form in mid-1941. The two-seat Il-2m3 was introduced in 1942, with a gunner for rear defence. The Shturmoviks fought against the Nazi invaders in 1941–42, but it was during the great battles of the Soviet counter-offensive in 1943–44 that the aircraft became, in Stalin's words, "as necessary to the Red Army as air or bread".

Shturmoviks operated in vast numbers against German armour and troops; 2,817 were present at the start of the battle of Kursk. Although many of them were destroyed, they earned a fearsome reputation as tank-busters. German troops nicknamed this aerial plague the "Black Death". Many Il-2s were also used by the Soviet Navy, whose pilots adopted a skip-bombing technique, bouncing their bombs off the water and into the side of a ship.

"A fighter without a gun…is like an airplane without a wing."

BRIGADIER GENERAL ROBIN OLDS, US AIR FORCE

SPECIFICATION

POWERPLANT 1 x 1,750-hp Mikulin AM-38F 12-cylinder liquid-cooled vee-type engine (Il-2 Type 3)

WINGSPAN 14.6m (47ft 11in)

WING AREA 38.5sq m (414sq ft)

LENGTH 11.6m (38ft 3in)

GROSS WEIGHT 6,360kg (14,021lb)

CRUISING SPEED 275km/h (171mph)

SERVICE RANGE 685km (426 miles)

ACCOMMODATION 1 crew (Il-2); 2 crew (Il-2 Type 3)

FIRST FLIGHT October 1939 (TsKB-55 original two-seat prototype)

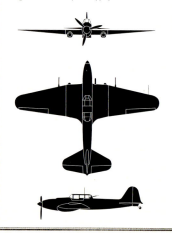

THE SHTURMOVIK PLAYED A LEADING ROLE IN THE GREAT BATTLES OF THE SOVIET COUNTER-OFFENSIVE IN 1943–44

THE STREAMLINED Fw 190 WAS FAST, STRONG, AND HEAVILY ARMED, MAKING IT GERMANY'S BEST FIGHTER IN WWII

FOCKE-WULF Fw 190

Designed by Kurt Tank, the Fw 190 is considered Germany's best single-seat fighter of World War II. When the first production model, the Fw 190A-1, entered Luftwaffe service in mid-1941, it took Allied intelligence completely by surprise because its air-cooled BMW radial engine gave it the appearance of an American fighter rather than a German one.

Disturbingly for the RAF, the Fw 190 proved clearly superior to the Spitfire Mk V, which was Britain's premier fighter at the time. It also outclassed the Messerschmitt Bf 109 in range and armament. The principal early version, the Fw 190A-8, carried two machine guns in front of the cockpit and four cannon in the wings. The aircraft proved exceptionally versatile, functioning in different versions as a fighter-bomber, ground-attack aircraft, torpedo bomber, or radar-equipped nightfighter.

It played a leading role in Germany's defence against Allied bombers, while on the Eastern Front it was used primarily in support of ground forces. In later models, the radial engine was replaced by a Junkers Jumo 213A in-line fitted with an annular radiator. This allowed the aircraft to operate up to a ceiling of 39,370 feet in its Fw 190D-9 form. Throughout the war, the Focke-Wulf remained the German fighter most feared and respected by Allied airmen.

"I can see them. High in the sun…their presence only betrayed by the reflected sparkle from highly polished windscreens and cockpit covers. 'They're coming down, Dogsbody. Break left'."

JOHNNIE JOHNSON, ON AN ENCOUNTER WITH GERMAN FIGHTERS IN *WING LEADER*, 1956

SPECIFICATION

POWERPLANT 1 × 1,700-hp BMW 801D-2 14-cylinder two-row radial engine (Fw 190 A-3)

WINGSPAN 10.4m (34ft ¾in)

WING AREA 18.3sq m (197sq ft)

LENGTH 8.8m (28ft 10½in)

GROSS WEIGHT 3,980kg (8,770lb)

MAXIMUM SPEED 502km/h at 6,000m (312mph at 19,685ft)

RANGE 800km (497 miles)

ACCOMMODATION 1 crew

FIRST FLIGHT 1 June 1939 (Fw 190 V-1 prototype)

BRISTOL BEAUFIGHTER

Bristol's pugnacious Type 156 Beaufighter was a heavy two-seater, long-range fighter that proved a formidable night interceptor and anti-shipping aircraft. A hastily improvised concept combining the flying surfaces and rear fuselage of the Beaufort torpedo bomber with a new front fuselage and higher-powered engines, the Beaufighter progressed from design to prototype in just six months.

The Mk 1F nightfighter entered service in August 1940, just in time for the start of the Luftwaffe's Blitz raids on British cities. Using airborne interception (AI) radar, the Beaufighter destroyed numerous German night raiders with its four 20mm canon. From December 1940 Beaufighter Mark ICs became RAF Coastal Command's standard long-range fighters. The most widely used Beaufighter variant, the TF. Mark X, carried out devastating attacks against enemy shipping after entering service in June 1943. It could be armed with bombs, rockets, or torpedoes, or a combination of all three.

Beaufighters also made effective ground-attack aircraft, operating in this role in the Western Desert and the Far East. Of the 5,564 Beaufighters delivered to the RAF, 2,205 were Mark Xs. Some 364 Beaufighters were built in Australia and operated by the Royal Australian Air Force against Japanese shipping around New Guinea.

"The Beaus came on, cannons blazing, while the hit ships…spurted defiant salvoes of flak. It was all over incredibly quickly. I had never before seen it quite so closely or so intensely as this…war!"

COLIN HODGKINSON, FIGHTER PILOT, WRITING IN *BEST FOOT FORWARD*, 1957

SPECIFICATION

POWERPLANT 2 × 1,670-hp Bristol Hercules VI or XVI 14-cylinder radial engines (Beaufighter Mk VI)

WINGSPAN 17.6m (57ft 10in)

WING AREA 46.7sq m (503sq ft)

LENGTH 12.7m (41ft 8in)

GROSS WEIGHT 9,798kg (21,600lb)

MAXIMUM SPEED 536km/h at 4,755m (333mph at 15,600ft)

RANGE Approx. 2,414km (1,500 miles)

ACCOMMODATION 2 crew

FIRST FLIGHT 17 July 1939

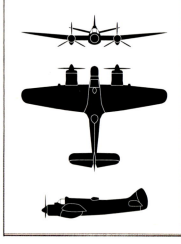

A HIGH-PERFORMANCE LONG-RANGE FIGHTER, THE BEAUFIGHTER ATTACKED BOTH SHIPPING AND GROUND FORCES

CONSOLIDATED B-24 LIBERATOR

More Consolidated B-24 Liberator bombers were built during World War II than any other American aircraft. The Liberator's most striking feature was a high-mounted, high-speed wing that reduced drag and contributed to the aircraft's exceptional range. Also, the two-section bomb bay in its fuselage accommodated an 8,000lb bombload – double that of a B-17.

The Liberator was used for reconnaissance, transport, and maritime patrol duties, as well as bombing missions. It was extensively employed in the Pacific War, but its most vital contribution was to the war against Germany.

RAF Coastal Command used the Liberator as an anti-submarine aircraft in the Battle of the Atlantic. The aircraft's range enabled it to bridge the mid-Atlantic gap during aerial patrols, helping to defend merchant convoys. The Liberator's range was also put to use in American raids on oilfields in Romania, vital to the German war effort: throughout 1944 the US Army Air Force (USAAF) carried out attacks from Italy that effectively ended oil production. In total, 18,188 Liberators were built.

"I had a ringside seat for the bombing. Straddled my parachute and looked down through the glass. Man oh man did they smash the hell out of that target."

RAY J. DUNPHY, B-24 NAVIGATOR, MISSION DIARY ENTRY, 1943

THE LIBERATOR HAD A DEEP FUSELAGE AND A HIGH-MOUNTED WING

SPECIFICATION

POWERPLANT 4 × 1,200-hp Pratt & Whitney R-1830-65 Twin Wasp 14-cylinder air-cooled radial engines (B-24 J)

WINGSPAN 33.5m (110ft)

WING AREA 97.4sq m (1,048sq ft)

LENGTH 20.5m (67ft 2in)

GROSS WEIGHT 29,478kg (65,000lb)

CRUISING SPEED 478km/h at 7,620m (297mph at 25,000ft)

RANGE 2,480km (1,540 miles)

ACCOMMODATION 7–10 crew

FIRST FLIGHT 29 December 1939 (XB-24)

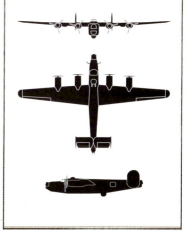

HEINKEL He 178

The Heinkel He 178 was the world's first aeroplane to fly purely on turbojet power. It was an experimental prototype built to test the feasibility of the jet engine developed by Dr Hans von Ohain. Apart from its powerplant, it was a conventionally designed, small monoplane with a duralumin fuselage and a mainly wooden wing.

The engine's air intake was located in the nose. The engine itself was set behind the cockpit and expelled its gases through a pipe that exited aft of the tail surfaces. In common with propeller-driven aircraft, the He 178 had a tailwheel – no one had realized at the time that jets would need a nosewheel, thereby raising the tail and keeping the jet efflux off the runway.

Although the He 178's maiden flight was in August 1938, it was not demonstrated officially until its second flight on 1 November 1939. By then its original HeS 3b engine had been replaced by the improved HeS 6, giving 1,300lb thrust. Unfortunately, the aircraft proved directionally unstable at high speed and its overall performance was disappointing. Although it attracted serious interest from the Nazi regime, Heinkel decided against trying to resolve the aircraft's problems. Instead, the company moved on to developing a twin-engine jet fighter.

SPECIFICATION

POWERPLANT 1 × 500kg (1,102lb) thrust HeS 3b petrol-burning turbojet engine

WINGSPAN 7.2m (23ft 7½in)

WING AREA 7.9sq m (85sq ft)

LENGTH 7.5m (24ft 6½in)

GROSS WEIGHT 1,988kg (4,383lb)

MAXIMUM SPEED 632km/h (393mph) at sea level

ACCOMMODATION 1 crew

FIRST FLIGHT 27 August 1939

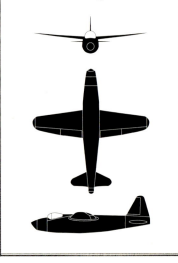

"A few minutes passed while he ogled the Heinkel, flying…below; it had not noticed him. What to do? Perhaps it was better not to rush the attack… Moreover, the BBC were just at that moment playing 'Plenty of time', a very fitting song it seemed."

RICHARD TOWNSEND BICKERS, AUTHOR, WRITING IN *GINGER LACEY: FIGHTER PILOT*

THE He 178 WAS THE FIRST AEROPLANE EVER TO FLY ON TURBOJET POWER ALONE

The Boeing B-17 Flying Fortress *Yankee Doodle* of the United States Army Air Forces' Eighth Air Force is tended by ground crew in Britain in preparation for another mission over enemy-occupied continental Europe during 1942.

THE MOST FAMOUS OF ALL JAPANESE COMBAT AIRCRAFT, THE ZERO INITIALLY OUTCLASSED EVERY ALLIED FIGHTER IN THE PACIFIC

MITSUBISHI A6M ZERO

The Japanese Navy's agile A6M Reisen "Zero" fighter thoroughly deserved the legendary status it acquired in the epic carrier battles of the Pacific War. Designed by Jiro Horikoshi, the single-seat aircraft was optimized for manoeuvrability and range. It had excellent aerodynamics and was lightweight, its skinning and main spar being made from the new extra-super-duralumin alloy. The armament was impressive, with two 20mm cannon in the wings and two machine guns above the engine.

Introduced in 1940, the Zero easily outclassed opposing Soviet and American fighters in combat over China. Its extraordinary range made it well suited for bomber escort work, a role it performed on 7 December 1941 when Zeros accompanied the force that struck Pearl Harbor. Faster, more manoeuvrable, and better armed than US Navy fighters, the Zero took a heavy toll of American aircraft during the Battle of Midway in June 1942. But after that point the Japanese fighters were outstripped by a new generation of US carrier aircraft.

Although later models were equipped with armour protection for the pilot and self-sealing fuel tanks to improve survivability, by 1944 they were being thrown away in kamikaze attacks. In total, 10,449 Zeros were built before Japan's defeat finally ended production in 1945.

SPECIFICATION

POWERPLANT 1 × 1,130-hp Nakajima Sakae 21 14-cylinder radial engine (A6M5)

WINGSPAN 11m (36ft 1in)

WING AREA 21.3sq m (230sq ft)

LENGTH 9.1m (29ft 11in)

GROSS WEIGHT 2,733kg (6,025lb)

MAXIMUM SPEED 565km/h at 6,000m (351mph at 19,700ft)

RANGE 1,925km (1,196 miles)

ACCOMMODATION 1 crew

FIRST FLIGHT 1 April 1939 (A6M1)

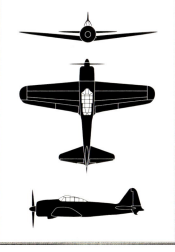

"…to fly is just like swimming. You do not forget easily….If I close my eyes…I can again feel the stick in my right hand, the throttle in my left, the rudder bar beneath my feet. I can sense the freedom…."

SABURO SAKAI, JAPANESE WORLD WAR II ACE

DE HAVILLAND MOSQUITO

Originally designed as a high-speed unarmed light bomber, the de Havilland D.H.98 Mosquito proved one of the most versatile aeroplanes of World War II, serving in a wide variety of roles, and excelling at each and every one.

The Mosquito was built almost entirely of plywood, sparing the use of metals that were then in short supply. From the maiden flight of its first prototype in November 1940 onwards, it demonstrated exceptional speed and agility on the power of its two Rolls-Royce Merlin engines.

Mosquitoes formed the core of RAF Bomber Command's Pathfinder Force, flying ahead of heavy night-bomber formations to mark targets with flares and operating Oboe radio-guidance equipment. The Mosquitoes also carried out many precision raids in their own right, relying on their speed for survival. Enemy fighters found them almost impossible to catch – Nazi air supremo, Hermann Göring, said the Mosquito's performance made him "green and yellow with envy".

A reconnaissance version of the aircraft took many vital photographs at both high and low altitudes, while Mosquito fighter-bombers served as rocket-firing close-support aircraft, as anti-shipping aircraft, as radar-equipped nightfighters, and as ground-attack aircraft striking enemy communications and supply lines. The "Wooden Wonder" continued in RAF service right up until the mid-1950s.

SPECIFICATION

POWERPLANT 2 × 1,620-hp Rolls-Royce Merlin 25 12-cylinder liquid-cooled vee engines (FB.Mk VI)

WINGSPAN 16.5m (54ft 2in)

WING AREA 42.2sq m (454sq ft)

LENGTH 12.5m (40ft 10¾in)

GROSS WEIGHT 10,115kg (22,300lb)

MAXIMUM SPEED 583km/h at 1,675m (362mph at 5,500ft)

RANGE 2,655km (1,650 miles) with internal bombload

ACCOMMODATION 2 crew

FIRST FLIGHT 25 November 1940

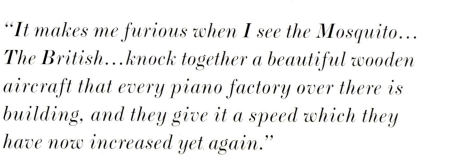

"It makes me furious when I see the Mosquito… The British…knock together a beautiful wooden aircraft that every piano factory over there is building, and they give it a speed which they have now increased yet again."

HERMANN GÖRING, COMMANDER OF THE LUFTWAFFE

A LIGHT, HIGH-SPEED FIGHTER-BOMBER, THE MOSQUITO WAS ONE OF THE OUTSTANDING AEROPLANES OF WORLD WAR II

RENOWNED FOR ITS PERFORMANCE, THE MUSTANG GAVE ALLIED BOMBERS AN EFFECTIVE ESCORT TO TARGETS DEEP INSIDE GERMANY

NORTH AMERICAN P-51 MUSTANG

Ultimately the greatest long-range fighter of World War II, the P-51 Mustang took some time to find its war-winning final shape. Designed in 1940 to meet an urgent British requirement for an aircraft to equip RAF Fighter Command, it initially proved a partial failure. The advanced laminar-flow wings and streamlined all-metal fuselage made the aircraft fast in low-level flight, but its Allison engine performed poorly at higher altitude.

Although the RAF deployed the Mustang as a ground-attack aircraft, it found it useless as an air-superiority fighter. Hoping to improve the aircraft's high-altitude performance, the British finally thought to test it with a Rolls-Royce Merlin engine.

The results were spectacular. When the US aircraft company North American fitted a Packard-built Merlin engine as standard in 1943, a great aircraft was born.

The Merlin-engined Mustang answered Allied bomber crews' prayers for a really effective fighter that would protect them in the dangerous skies over Germany. With fuel drop tanks, the Mustangs could escort bombers all the way to Berlin and back. Fast and agile, they could outfight any German interceptor sent up against them, even when operating at extreme range. The Mustang was still the US's frontline fighter at the start of the Korean War in 1950. More than 15,000 of the aircraft were built in total.

> *"I consider the P-51 the best battle horse you had of all the fighter escorts."*
>
> GÜNTHER RALL, LUFTWAFFE, ON ALLIED AIRCRAFT DURING WWII

SPECIFICATION

POWERPLANT 1 x 1,490-hp Packard-built V-1650-7 Rolls-Royce Merlin V12 liquid-cooled engine (P-51D)

WINGSPAN 11.9m (37ft ¼in)

WING AREA 21.7sq m (233sq ft)

LENGTH 9.8m (32ft 3in)

GROSS WEIGHT 5,490kg (12,100lb)

MAXIMUM SPEED 704km/h at 7,630m (437mph at 25,000ft)

RANGE 3,380km (2,100 miles) with maximum external fuel

ACCOMMODATION 1 crew

FIRST FLIGHT 25 October 1940 (NA-73X prototype) machine guns

VOUGHT F4U CORSAIR

The American F4U Corsair is widely acknowledged as the outstanding carrier-borne fighter of World War II. Its most distinctive feature was the inverted-gull wing. This was ingeniously designed to allow the undercarriage, fitted at the lowest point of the wing, to be short and sturdy – and thus ideal for carrier landing – while still providing adequate ground clearance for the large-diameter propeller. The wing shape had the side-effect of creating a whistling sound in flight – hence the Japanese nickname for the aircraft, "the Whistling Death".

The Corsair was far from problem-free. The long radial engine in front of the pilot dangerously obscured his view of the deck when coming in to land. The aircraft was consequently first deployed as a shore-based fighter with the US Marines. Eventually, the cockpit was raised to improve the pilot's view, but Corsairs did not operate from carriers until April 1944, almost four years after the prototype's maiden flight.

The aircraft's sterling performance more than compensated for the long delay. In air combat in the Pacific, on average 11 Zeros or other Japanese fighter planes were shot down for every Corsair that was lost. The F4U also proved an excellent strike aircraft, armed with bombs or rockets. Of the 12,571 Corsairs built, more than 2,000 served with Britain's Fleet Air Arm.

"It got to be a very fine plane once the bugs were out of it."

HERBERT D. RILEY, ADMIRAL, US NAVY, ON THE F4U CORSAIR

SPECIFICATION

POWERPLANT 1 × 2,000-hp Pratt & Whitney R-2800-8 Double Wasp 18-cylinder radial engine (F4U-1)

WINGSPAN 12.5m (40ft 11¾in)

WING AREA 29.2sq m (314sq ft)

LENGTH 10m (32ft 9½in)

GROSS WEIGHT 6,280kg (13,846lb)

MAXIMUM SPEED 671km/h at 6,066m (417mph at 19,900ft)

RANGE 1,633km (1,015 miles)

ACCOMMODATION 1 crew

FIRST FLIGHT 29 May 1940

THE F4U HAD A DISTINCTIVE INVERTED-GULL WING THAT ALLOWED A SHORTER UNDERCARRIAGE TO BE USED

AVRO LANCASTER

When the first Lancasters appeared at RAF Bomber Command bases in the spring of 1942, they were greeted with relief and enthusiasm by aircrews. Here at last was an aircraft truly fitted for the role of night-time heavy bomber.

Designed by Roy Chadwick and powered by four Merlin engines, the Lancaster could carry a standard bombload more than double that of the Boeing B-17. It had fewer guns than the US's day bombers, but powered turrets in the nose, upper fuselage, and tail provided solid defence against nightfighters.

As the war progressed, Lancasters were packed with navigational and electronic warfare equipment, making them sophisticated fighting machines. Yet it was their ability to absorb punishment and their sheer power that most impressed. The Lancaster was the only RAF bomber able to carry the 12,000lb Tallboy bomb and a modified late model dropped the massive 22,000lb Grand Slam bomb in 1945.

The most celebrated of the Lancasters' 156,000 sorties, however, was 617 Squadron's "Dambuster" raid against the Ruhr dams in May 1943, using Barnes Wallis's "bouncing bombs". That mission alone sufficed to make the powerful aircraft an aviation legend.

> *"We saw them coming like relief coming to a hard-pressed army; they were unconquerable; the days of heavy losses were over."*
>
> DON CHARLWOOD, RAF, RECALLING THE LANCASTER

LANCASTERS TOOK PART IN THE LEGENDARY "DAMBUSTER" RAID OF 1943

SPECIFICATION

POWERPLANT 4 x 1,640-hp Rolls-Royce Merlin XXIV 12-cylinder liquid-cooled vee engines (B Mk I)

WINGSPAN 31.1m (102ft)

WING AREA 120.5sq m (1,297sq ft)

LENGTH 21.2m (69ft 6in)

GROSS WEIGHT 31,751kg (70,000lb)

CRUISING SPEED 338km/h at 6,100m (210mph at 20,000ft)

RANGE 4,072km with a 3,175kg (2,530 miles with a 7,000lb) bombload

ACCOMMODATION 7 crew

FIRST FLIGHT 9 January 1941

LAVOCHKIN LaGG-3

It is incredible that 6,528 Lavochkin LaGG-3 fighters were built in the Soviet Union between 1941 and late 1943, because the aeroplane was dreadful. First flown in December 1940, and hastily rushed into production, it was derived from Semyon Lavochkin's slightly earlier LaGG-1. It had a wooden, semi-monocoque fuselage skinned with glued layers of birch veneer and plywood, as were its wings and tail surfaces. A composite phenol-impregnated wood was used for the main spars and local reinforcement.

The LaGG-1 exhibited 115 faults and defects during official tests, and although some were rectified, many more were carried over into the LaGG-3, and even got worse.

The aircraft became substantially heavier and its performance deteriorated. It had poor manoeuvrability and a nasty tendency to go into an often-fatal spin. The engine overheated, the radiators and hydraulics leaked, linkages in the control system failed, and the undercarriage tended to collapse.

Although some improvements were carried out, Soviet pilots dubbed the aircraft the "Mortician's Friend". Yet despite this, in early May 1942 a third of all the fighters in Soviet service were LaGG-3s. Lavochkin eventually solved some of the worst performance defects by replacing the in-line engine with a radial powerplant, creating the considerably more effective La-5.

"I chased a Lavochkin a great distance at full throttle and I still could not get him. He was damned fast."

GÜNTHER RALL, LUFTWAFFE, WWII

SPECIFICATION

POWERPLANT 1 x 1,180-hp Klimov M-105PF 12-cylinder liquid-cooled vee engine (LaGG-3 Oblegchenniy – boosted and lightened from July–August 1942)

WINGSPAN 9.8m (32ft 1¾in)

WING AREA 17.5sq m (189sq ft)

LENGTH 8.9m (29ft 2½in)

GROSS WEIGHT 2,911kg (6,418lb)

MAXIMUM SPEED 565km/h at 5,000m (351mph at 16,404ft)

RANGE 650km (404 miles)

ACCOMMODATION 1 crew

FIRST FLIGHT 30 March 1940 (I-301 LaGG-1 the LaGG-3 prototype)

THE LaGG-3's POOR PERFORMANCE AND TENDENCY TO GO INTO A FATAL SPIN EARNED IT THE NICKNAME "THE MORTICIAN'S FRIEND"

THE COMPACT GLOSTER-WHITTLE E.28/39 WAS THE FIRST JET AEROPLANE TO TAKE TO THE SKIES OVER BRITAIN

GLOSTER-WHITTLE E.28/39

The Gloster-Whittle E.28/39 was the first jet aeroplane to fly in Britain. It was built to test the viability of the turbojet engine invented by Flight Lieutenant Frank Whittle. Apart from its powerplant, the aircraft, designed by George Carter of Gloster Aircraft, was thoroughly conventional.

It was a compact all-metal single-seater with a monocoque fuselage, a low wing, and a short, retractable tricycle undercarriage. The cockpit was a little way back from the nose air intake, and the engine was housed behind it, with a long exhaust pipe running to the jet orifice in the tail.

After initial taxiing tests and short hops with a "ground-running" engine, the maiden flight took place on the evening of 15 May 1941. Test pilot Flight Lieutenant Gerry Sayer kept the aircraft in the air for 17 minutes, without incident. Over the next 13 days, the prototype clocked up ten hours of flying time without needing to remove the engine cover. Test flights continued for the next three years. A second protoype joined the test programme in March 1943, but was destroyed in an accident the following July.

The Gloster company used the experience gained from these experimental flights to create the Meteor, Britain's first jet fighter, some of which flew in 1945. The original E.28/39 is now an exhibit at the Science Museum in London.

"It's only the beginning but the implications are terrific."

GERALD SAYER, FIRST FLIGHT IN THE GLOSTER-WHITTLE E.28/39

SPECIFICATION

POWERPLANT 1 x 798kg (1,760lb) thrust Power Jets W.2/500 turbojet engine

WINGSPAN 8.8m (29ft)

WING AREA 13.6sq m (147sq ft)

LENGTH 7.7m (25ft 3¾in)

GROSS WEIGHT 1,700kg (3,748lb)

MAXIMUM SPEED 750km/h at 3,048m (466mph at 10,000ft)

ACCOMMODATION 1 crew

FIRST FLIGHT 15 May 1941

Groundcrew servicing American Republic P-47 Thunderbolt fighter-bombers serving with the RAF on the Arakan Front in Burma in 1944 turn to watch as three sister P-47s make a fly-over. The aircrafts' long-range underwing fuel tanks are clearly visible.

MESSERSCHMITT Me 323 GIGANT

One of the largest aircraft to fly in World War II, the aptly-named Gigant ("Giant") was a lumbering beast of ungainly appearance, but it gave the German Army the heavy-lift transport it desperately needed.

The aircraft was derived from an assault glider, the massive Me 321, designed by Messerschmitt for the invasion of the Soviet Union in 1941. There were so many accidents towing the heavy-lift glider that Messerschmitt decided to develop a powered version, the Me 323.

Initially the Gigant was fitted with four engines, but this proved inadequate to power the monster, which required six – and even then sometimes had to resort to rocket-assisted take-off. Loads were taken aboard through enormous clamshell nose doors and a ten-wheel bogie-type undercarriage allowed the aircraft to land even on rough airstrips.

The first operational Me 323 unit was formed in the Middle East in November 1942, in time to ferry retreating German forces from Tunisia to Sicily. It also served extensively on the Eastern Front. However, the Gigant proved extremely vulnerable to enemy fighters. Successive models bristled with ever more guns – mounted in the nose, on the wings, and at the rear of the engine nacelles, as well as poking out from every available point on the fuselage. Yet, whole fleets of Me 323s were nonetheless shot down.

> *"Gliders… [will be] the freight trains of the air."*
>
> GROVER LOENING, US AVIATION PIONEER, 1944

SPECIFICATION

POWERPLANT 6 × 1,140-hp Gnome-Rhône 14N 14-cylinder radial engines (Me 323 E-2)

WINGSPAN 55m (180ft 5½in)

WING AREA 300sq m (3,229sq ft)

LENGTH 28.5m (93ft 6in)

GROSS WEIGHT 45,000kg (99,210lb)

CRUISING SPEED 225km/h (140mph) at sea level

RANGE 1,300km (808 miles)

ACCOMMODATION 5 crew, up to 120 fully equipped troops, or 9,765kg (21,500lb) of freight

FIRST FLIGHT Autumn 1941 (Me 321 transport glider 25 February 1941)

THE MASSIVE GIGANT PROVIDED THE GERMAN ARMY WITH HEAVY-LIFT TRANSPORT BUT PROVED TOO VULNERABLE TO ENEMY FIRE

THE FIRST OPERATIONAL JET FIGHTER, THE Me 262 SCHWALBE WAS EXTREMELY FAST AND AN EXCELLENT INTERCEPTOR

MESSERSCHMITT Me 262 SCHWALBE

The shark-like Messerschmitt Me 262 Schwalbe was the world's first operational jet fighter. Powered by two Junkers Jumo engines mounted under its slightly swept-back wings, it was at least 70mph faster than any World War II piston-engine aircraft. German pilot, Adolf Galland, described the exhilarating experience of flying the jet as like being "pushed by angels".

Unfortunately for the Luftwaffe, the development of the Me 262 was slow. The first prototypes were ready by 1941, but there was no suitable jet engine, so they made their maiden flight with a propeller. After the Me 262 made its first jet-powered flight in July 1942, further delays ensued due to Hitler's efforts to have the aircraft developed as a bomber instead of a fighter.

When Schwalbes were belatedly added to the defence of Germany in 1944–45, they brought down a fair number of Allied bombers. Their speed made them excellent interceptors, especially when armed with air-to-air rockets, but they were not agile enough to match Allied fighters in a dogfight.

Essentially still experimental aircraft, the Me 262s were subject to frequent engine flame-outs and were a nightmare to land, the touchdown speed being far too high for safety. They were never available in sufficient numbers to have a serious effect on the air war, and only some 300 ever saw combat.

"For the first time I was flying by jet propulsion. No engine vibrations. No torque and no lashing sound of the propeller. Accompanied by a whistling sound, my jet shot through the air."

ADOLF GALLAND, ON FLYING THE Me 262, 1943

SPECIFICATION

POWERPLANT 2 x 900kg (1,984lb) thrust Junkers Jumo 004 B turbojet engines (Me 262A-1a)

WINGSPAN 12.6m (41ft 2½in)

WING AREA 21.7sq m (234sq ft)

LENGTH 10.6m (34ft 7¼in)

GROSS WEIGHT 6,074kg (13,391lb)

MAXIMUM SPEED 870km/h at 6,000m (541mph at 19,685ft)

RANGE 600km (373 miles)

ACCOMMODATION 1 crew

FIRST FLIGHT 18 April 1941 (V1 prototype with a piston engine)

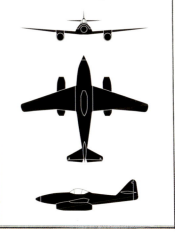

MESSERSCHMITT Me 163 KOMET

The Me 163 Komet was the only German rocket-powered aircraft used in World War II. It evolved from Dr Alexander Lippisch's experiments with tailless gliders. In summer 1941 a Walter rocket motor, powered by liquid propellants, was installed on one of Lippisch's protoypes and flight-tested at Peenemunde on the Baltic.

The aircraft's remarkable performance led to the development of the larger Me 163B, with a more powerful motor using a volatile combination of hydrogen peroxide and phosphate ("*T-Stoff*"), and of calcium permanganate, hydrazine hydrate, and methanol ("*C-Stoff*").

The Komet was first delivered to Luftwaffe units in May 1944, to be used as a point-defence interceptor against Allied daylight bombers. The aircraft did not have a conventional undercarriage. It took off on a two-wheel trolley that was jettisoned as it left the ground, and then landed on a sprung central skid.

The Komet's speed and rate of climb were phenomenal, but it was only capable of making brief sorties. Pilots found that they closed with their target so quickly that they had little chance of using their heavy twin cannon effectively. Worst of all, the fuel had a regrettable tendency to explode, especially on landing, and could dissolve anything organic, forcing the pilots to wear protective suits. Although some 400 Komets were built, only a few saw combat.

"As long as I look into the muzzles, nothing can happen to me. Only if he pulls lead am I in danger."

CAPTAIN HANS-JOACHIM MARSEILLE, LUFTWAFFE

SPECIFICATION

POWERPLANT 1 x 1,700kg (3,750lb) thrust Walter HWK 509A-2 bi-fuel rocket motor (Me 163B-1a)

WINGSPAN 9.3m (30ft 7in)

WING AREA 18.5sq m (199sq ft)

LENGTH 15.8m (19ft 2in)

GROSS WEIGHT 4,110kg (9,061lb)

MAXIMUM SPEED 960km/h at 10,000m (596mph at 32,810ft)

ENDURANCE 7 minutes and 30 seconds at maximum power

ACCOMMODATION 1 crew

FIRST FLIGHT 13 February 1941 (towed flight Me 163A V4), 13 August 1941 (powered flight Me 163A V4)

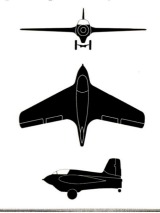

A REVOLUTIONARY ROCKET-POWERED INTERCEPTOR, THE Me 163 KOMET COULD CLIMB WITH PHENOMENAL SPEED

SOLID AND RELIABLE, THE C-54 SKYMASTER PLAYED A VITAL ROLE IN TRANSPORTING SOLDIERS AND SUPPLIES AROUND THE WORLD

DOUGLAS C-54 SKYMASTER

While never the most glamorous of military aeroplanes, transport aircraft are often the most vital. The ever-reliable C-54 Skymaster ferried soldiers and supplies across oceans and continents throughout World War II and for many years after.

The original C-54s were simply Douglas DC-4 airliners converted for military use. Developed as the successor to the DC-3, with much greater carrying capacity and range, the DC-4 was just entering production when the Japanese attacked Pearl Harbor. The US Army Air Force (USAAF) commandeered the production line and the first batch of airliners thus became the US's first four-engine military transports. Subsequent C-54s were modified to carry heavy freight, with increased fuel capacity, a strengthened floor, a large door, a hoist and winch, and a cabin that could be converted for troops or cargo.

Operated by Air Transport Command, the C-54 served worldwide, establishing an unsurpassed safety record. It was the first transport aircraft to establish regular services across the North Atlantic and the Pacific and Indian Oceans; only three were lost in 79,642 ocean crossings. One C-54, nicknamed the "Sacred Cow", was fitted out as a presidential aircraft – the forerunner of Air Force One. Postwar, C-54s played prominent roles in the Berlin Airlift and the Korean War. They remained in service into the 1960s.

"I was touched...when we first climbed aboard. There, on the bulkhead...was a note...It said 'God bless you son,' and was signed 'Rosie', the universal name for the women factory workers who assembled America's aircraft in the 1940's."

CLYDE HUSSEY, USAF RADIO OPERATOR, WORLD WAR II.

SPECIFICATION

POWERPLANT 4 x 1,435-hp Pratt & Whitney R-2000-9 Twin Wasp radial engines

WINGSPAN 35.8m (117ft 6in)

WING AREA 136.9sq m (1,463sq ft)

LENGTH 28.6m (93ft 11in)

GROSS WEIGHT 33,112kg (73,000lb)

MAXIMUM SPEED 440km/h (273mph)

RANGE 6,240km (3,877 miles)

ACCOMMODATION 4 crew, 26 passengers, or cargo payload up to 9,979kg (22,000lb)

FIRST FLIGHT 14 February 1942

GLOSTER METEOR

Because of the surprising tardiness of the US's development of jet-propelled aircraft, the RAF's Gloster Meteor was the sole Allied jet to enter combat during World War II. The first Meteors were delivered to 616 Squadron in July 1944, and quickly found vital employment intercepting German V1 flying bombs targeted at London.

This was an ideal use for the Meteor's speed, which was its single outstanding advantage over piston-engined fighters. Being a lot quicker than the V1s, Meteors had considerable success in shooting them down over open countryside, using their nose-mounted 20mm Hispano guns. Some Meteors also reportedly went wingtip to wingtip with the flying bombs, toppling their stabilizing gyros with a nifty flick.

In early 1945 some of the jets were sent to Belgium to help resist a German air offensive that never came. By the end of the war no Meteor had yet shot down a piloted enemy in air-to-air combat, although they did destroy Luftwaffe aircraft on the ground in strafing attacks. Postwar, the much-improved Meteor F.8, with a bubble cockpit and increased fuel capacity, entered service in 1950 and fought with United Nations forces in Korea. Meteors were finally withdrawn from front-line RAF service in 1960.

"The most important thing to a fighter pilot is speed. The faster an aircraft is moving when he spots an enemy aircraft, the sooner he will be able to take the bounce and get to the Hun."

DUANE W. BEESON, WWII PILOT

SPECIFICATION

POWERPLANT 2 x 906kg (2,000lb) thrust Rolls-Royce Derwent 1 turbojet engines (F Mk III)

WINGSPAN 13.1m (43ft)

WING AREA 34.7sq m (374sq ft)

LENGTH 12.5m (41ft)

GROSS WEIGHT 6,314kg (13,920lb)

MAXIMUM SPEED 668km/h at 3,048m (415mph at 10,000ft)

RANGE 1,580km (982 miles)

ACCOMMODATION 1 crew

FIRST FLIGHT 5 March 1943 (powered by two Halford H.1 engines of 1,500lb [680kg] thrust)

THE GLOSTER METEOR WAS THE FIRST BRITISH JET FIGHTER AND THE ONLY ALLIED JET TO GO INTO COMBAT DURING WORLD WAR II

AN ADVANCED HIGH-ALTITUDE BOMBER, THE B-29 SUPERFORTRESS DEVASTATED THE CITIES OF JAPAN AT THE END OF WORLD WAR II

BOEING B-29 SUPERFORTRESS

The Boeing B-29 was the aircraft that dropped atomic bombs on Hiroshima and Nagasaki. The most advanced bomber to enter service in World War II, it surpassed all its predecessors in range, speed, payload, and the comfort it accorded its crew. Its pressurized and heated cabins completely transformed the experience of high-altitude bombing missions.

Except for a manned tail turret, the aircraft's guns were operated from a central position by remote control using computerized sights. The front and rear compartments in the tubular fuselage were connected by a long tunnel passing over twin bomb bays.

The B-29s were devoted exclusively to the Pacific Theatre. They made their first raids on Japan in June 1944, flying from bases in India via southwest China. The aircraft had been rushed into service and showed some alarming teething troubles, including a spate of engine fires.

After the US Marines conquered the Marianas, the B-29s were able to launch a sustained bombing offensive from Pacific island bases. Their raids on Japanese cities became awesomely effective from March 1945, when high-altitude daylight bombing was replaced by night-time low-level incendiary attacks. A vast amount of devastation had already been caused by the time *Enola Gay* and *Bock's Car* dropped their city-destroying bombs on 6 and 9 August 1945, bringing the war to an abrupt end.

"We are returning from the longest, and probably the final, bombing mission of World War II...I have my headphones on, listening for the surrender message."

CLYDE HUSSEY, B.29 RADIO OPERATOR, WWII

SPECIFICATION

POWERPLANT 4 x 2,200-hp Wright R-3350-23 Double Cyclone 18-cylinder turbo-supercharged radial engines

WINGSPAN 43.1m (141ft 3in)

WING AREA 161.3sq m (1,736sq ft)

LENGTH 30.2m (99ft)

GROSS WEIGHT 47,628kg (105,000lb)

MAXIMUM SPEED 576km/h at 7,620m (358mph at 25,000ft)

RANGE 9,382km (5,830 miles)

ACCOMMODATION 10 crew

FIRST FLIGHT 21 September 1942

YOKOSUKA OHKA

Essentially a piloted flying bomb, the romantically named Ohka ("Cherry Blossom") was the only aircraft ever designed exclusively for suicide missions. It was deployed as part of the kamikaze campaign being mounted by Japanese pilots against Allied warships in the last year of the war.

Based on an original suggestion by Japanese naval transport pilot, Mitsuo Ohta, the Ohka was a rocket-propelled single-seater made of wood and non-critical metal alloys, with a warhead in its nose. It was taken aloft beneath a bomber aircraft – typically the twin-engine Mitsubishi G4M – and launched in the air once it was within range of its target. Its pilot glided downwards before igniting a trio of solid-propellant rocket motors in the tail for the final high-speed attack run, hoping to crash into the targeted ship and explode.

In the first attempted Ohka action, on 21 March 1945, the 16 parent aircraft were intercepted and forced to release their deadly load prematurely. Success came on 1 April, when the US battleship *West Virginia* and three transport vessels were damaged.

The first Allied ship sunk by Ohkas was the destroyer *Mannert L. Abele*, off Okinawa on 12 April. However, many Ohkas were destroyed on the ground or while they were still attached to their parent aircraft, so their desperate attacks did little to offset Allied aerial and naval supremacy.

"Mother... You have done a splendid job of raising me to become an honourable man... I will do a splendid job sinking an enemy aircraft carrier. Do brag about me."

ICHIZO HYASHI, KAMIKAZE PILOT, IN HIS FAREWELL LETTER

SPECIFICATION

POWERPLANT 3 × Type 4 Mark 1 Model 20 solid-fuel rockets with a combined thrust of 800kg (1,764lb) – (MXY7 Model 11)

WINGSPAN 5.1m (16ft 9½in)

WING AREA 6sq m (65sq ft)

LENGTH 6.1m (19ft 11in)

GROSS WEIGHT 2,140kg (4,718lb)

CRUISING SPEED 650km/h (404mph)

RANGE 37km (23 miles)

ACCOMMODATION 1 crew

FIRST FLIGHT Unpowered October 1944 (powered November 1944)

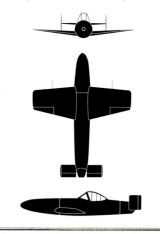

CHEAPLY PRODUCED, THE OHKA WAS A SINGLE-SEAT, ROCKET-PROPELLED FLYING BOMB PILOTED BY JAPANESE KAMIKAZE PILOTS

The vast patchwork of airfields that were a legacy of World War II rendered obsolete the commercial flying boats. They were replaced by multi-engined landplanes with pressurized passenger cabins, although these, too, soon gave way to the unprecedented speed and comfort of the first turboprop and pure-jet airliners. German wartime research into high-speed aerodynamics had pioneered innovations such as swept wings and podded engines, ushering in the era of supersonic flight. There was also tremendous experimentation with new technologies. In military aviation, the jet engine revolutionized the performance of front-line fighters and bombers, allowing them to climb higher and fly faster than ever before. The greatest developments of this era were supersonic transport aircraft, high-capacity widebody airliners, and vertical take-off aeroplanes. However, piston-engined aeroplanes were still widely used: as well as conducting survey and agricultural work, they were flown by smaller airlines which were being set up in previously remote parts of the world.

5

1946–1969

JOINING THE JET REVOLUTION

LOCKHEED CONSTELLATION

Known affectionately as the "Connie", the Lockheed Constellation was the most graceful of the great four-engine propliners that opened up intercontinental air routes in the immediate postwar years. With its flowing contours and distinctive triple tail, it had a supremely elegant exterior to match its stylish passenger accommodation.

Designed by Kelly Johnson, the Constellation originated in 1939 with a request from TWA for a large airliner with a pressurized cabin and supercharged engines.

War interrupted its development and, as a consequence, the Constellation first flew in 1943 as the C-69 military transport. Immediately after peace broke out, the aircraft was rushed into passenger service by TWA and a clutch of other airlines. TWA inaugurated the first transatlantic Constellation service between New York and Paris in February 1946, with intermediate stops at Gander, Newfoundland, and Shannon, Ireland.

The airliner's glamour was brilliantly matched by its performance, carrying up to 60 passengers from San Francisco to New York in 11 hours.

Over the following decade repeated upgrades of this magnificent aircraft progressively increased its range and payload, culminating in the L1649 Starliner of 1956, which could carry almost 100 passengers and fly from Los Angeles to London non-stop in just 19 hours.

"A commercial aircraft is a vehicle capable of supporting itself aerodynamically and economically at the same time."

WILLIAM B. STOUT, DESIGNER OF THE FORD TRI-MOTOR

SPECIFICATION

POWERPLANT 4 × 2,500-hp Wright Cyclone R-3350-C18-BD1 18-cylinder radial engines (L-749A)

WINGSPAN 37.5m (123ft)

LENGTH 29m (95ft 2in)

GROSS WEIGHT 48,534kg (107,000lb)

CRUISING SPEED 528km/h (328mph)

RANGE 5,890km (3,660 miles) New York to Paris non-stop

ACCOMMODATION 4–5 flight crew, 48–81 passengers, plus cabin crew

FIRST FLIGHT 9 January 1943 (Lockheed Model 49 – USAAF C-69)

A STYLISH FOUR-ENGINE PROPLINER, THE LOCKHEED CONSTELLATION OPENED UP POSTWAR INTERCONTINENTAL AIR ROUTES

THE HUGE H-4 HERCULES FLYING BOAT WAS BUILT BY HOWARD HUGHES BUT IT MADE ONLY ONE FLIGHT

HUGHES H-4 HERCULES

In 1942 American millionaire and aviation enthusiast, Howard Hughes, and ship-builder, Henry Kaiser, were jointly awarded $18 million of US government funding to build a "flying liberty ship".

This was to be a huge flying boat capable of ferrying American soldiers and military equipment across the Atlantic, free from the threat of German U-boats. Kaiser withdrew from the project when it was still in the design stage, leaving Hughes to complete the gargantuan aircraft on his own.

The H-4 Hercules was principally made of laminated birch, but the press, much to Hughes's annoyance, dubbed it the "Spruce Goose". With eight engines on its massive wing, it was by far the largest aircraft built until the late 1980s. It was intended to carry a payload of around 700 servicemen.

The war ended before the prototype was finished. In June 1946 its major components were moved from the Hughes Aircraft Company's factory to Long Beach, California, for final assembly.

The flying boat was finally launched on 1 November 1947, having cost Hughes some $5 million. The next day, with Hughes piloting, the Hercules lifted off the water and made a straight flight of about a mile at a height of 70–80 feet. No further flights were attempted. In September 1953 the H-4 was seriously damaged and it never flew again.

"Flying might not be all plain sailing, but the fun of it is worth the price."

AMELIA EARHART, AVIATRIX

SPECIFICATION

POWERPLANT 8 × 3,000-hp Pratt & Whitney R-4360 Wasp Major 28-cylinder radial engines

WINGSPAN 97.5m (320ft)

WING AREA 1,061.8sq m (11,429½sq ft)

LENGTH 66.8m (219ft)

GROSS WEIGHT Approx 181,440kg (400,000lb)

DESIGN CRUISING SPEED More than 322km/h (200mph)

PROJECTED RANGE 4,828km (3,000 miles)

ACCOMMODATION Crew and up to 700 passengers or equivalent freight

FIRST FLIGHT 2 November 1947

BELL X-1

The rocket-powered Bell X-1 was the first aircraft to fly at above the speed of sound. It was built expressly to investigate the problem of "breaking the sound barrier", then regarded with some trepidation.

The X-1 was straight-winged and aerodynamically clean, with a fuselage modelled along the lines of a 0.50-calibre bullet. For its experimental flights, it was carried aloft in the bomb-bay of a B-29 bomber and released at high altitude. Its four-chamber rocket motor used up its alcohol and liquid oxygen fuel in a few minutes, after which the aircraft was landed as a glider.

The X-1 made its first powered flight on 29 August 1947, piloted by Captain Charles "Chuck" Yeager. Although the cockpit was cramped, the aircraft proved docile and a pleasure to fly.

The big event came on 14 October 1947, on flight 50 of the test programme. Piloting an X-1 he had named *Glamorous Glennis*, in tribute to his wife, Yeager was released at 20,000ft, then ignited two chambers of the rocket motor for initial acceleration and climb. At 40,000 feet he levelled off and ignited the other two chambers.

Seconds later the Bell X-1 smoothly accelerated through Mach 1 – the speed of sound – to Mach 1.06. Ten minutes later Yeager was safely back on the ground, and history had been made.

SPECIFICATION

POWERPLANT 1 × 2,722kg (6,000lb) maximum static thrust Reaction Motors XLR11-RM-5 4-chamber bi-fuel (alcohol and liquid oxygen) rocket engine

WINGSPAN 8.5m (28ft)

LENGTH 9.5m (31ft)

GROSS WEIGHT 6,078kg (13,400lb)

MAXIMUM SPEED 1,609km/h at 18,288m (1,000mph at 60,000ft)

ENDURANCE 2½ minutes at maximum thrust

ACCOMMODATION 1 crew

FIRST FLIGHT 9 December 1946

"Suddenly the Mach needle…went up to .995 Mach – then tipped right off the scale…We were flying supersonic. And it was smooth as a baby's bottom."

GENERAL CHARLES "CHUCK" YEAGER, ON HIS FIRST SUPERSONIC FLIGHT IN THE BELL X-1

THE SLEEK, AERODYNAMICALLY CLEAN FUSELAGE OF THE SUPERSONIC BELL X-I RESEMBLED A 0.50-CALIBRE BULLET

THE EXTRAORDINARY YB-49 EXCELLED IN TESTS BUT WAS SHELVED AS MORE CONVENTIONAL DESIGNS FOUND FAVOUR

NORTHROP YB-49

Throughout his career, imaginative American designer Jack Northrop believed that the ultimate in aircraft development would be a "flying wing", with neither fuselage nor tail.

During World War II his company developed the massive XB-35 all-wing piston-engined bomber, but by the time it flew in 1946 the jet era had arrived. Northrop then built two jet-powered versions of the bomber, designated YB-49s.

This extraordinary aircraft was powered by eight Allison turbojets buried in the wing. Its two pilots sat beneath a large canopy offset to port; off to starboard, in the nose, there was a glazed area over the navigator's and bombardier's position. The two bomb bays were also contained in the wing.

Although it looked like a science fiction fantasy, the flying-wing bomber really worked. It did well in altitude, speed, and endurance tests, flying from California to Washington DC in 4 hours and 20 minutes. Its record was then marred when one of the machines broke up in flight, killing its crew.

Despite this, the US Air Force ordered 30 RB-49A reconnaissance bombers in 1948, only to cancel the order as more conventional designs won favour. The cancellation of the project was a personal tragedy for Northrop. By official order, all flying-wing airframes were broken up for scrap.

"In the case of pilots, it is a little touch of madness that drives us to go beyond all known bounds."

JACQUELINE AURIOL, TEST PILOT

SPECIFICATION

POWERPLANT 8 x 1,724kg (3,800lb) thrust Allison J35-A-15 turbojet engines

WINGSPAN 52.4m (172ft)

WING AREA 371.6sq m (4,000sq ft)

LENGTH 16.2m (53ft 1in)

GROSS WEIGHT 87,970kg (193,938lb)

MAXIMUM SPEED 793km/h (493mph)

COMBAT RANGE 2,599km (1,615 miles)

ACCOMMODATION 7 crew

FIRST FLIGHT 1 October 1947

BOEING B-47

The futuristic-looking B-47 Stratojet bomber formed the core of the United States's nuclear bomber force in the 1950s. It proved to be a revolutionary aircraft in both design and performance.

When Boeing set out to create a jet-powered multi-engine bomber for the US Army Air Force in 1944, the designers thought in terms of a straight-winged aeroplane such as the B-29 Superfortress. After the defeat of the Nazis in May 1945, however, they were able to examine German wartime research on jet aircraft and realized that a swept wing would be far more efficient at high subsonic speed.

A radical rethink produced the B-47, with a 35-degree swept wing mounted high on the fuselage and six jet engines housed in pods on underwing pylons. The bomber initially also had 18 rockets in the fuselage for assisted take-off, to blast it into the air when fully laden with bombs and fuel. A drag parachute deployed to slow the aircraft on landing.

The B-47 was astonishingly fast and it was confidently expected to survive on missions with minimal armament, due to its exceptional speed and altitude.

However, it was not entirely satisfactory, since it lacked the intercontinental range to carry out a strike on the Soviet Union directly from bases in the United States. This problem was eventually solved by the introduction of in-flight refuelling.

"There are two kinds of airplanes – those you fly and those that fly you... You must have a distinct understanding at the very start as to who is the boss."

ERNEST K. GANN, AVIATOR AND AUTHOR

SPECIFICATION

POWERPLANT 6 × 2,722kg (6,000lb) thrust General Electric J47-GE-25 turbojet engines (B-47E)

WINGSPAN 35.4m (116ft)

LENGTH 32.6m (107ft)

GROSS WEIGHT 90,720kg (200,000lb)

MAXIMUM SPEED More than 966km/h (600mph)

COMBAT RADIUS 3,240km (2,013 miles)

FIRST FLIGHT 17 December 1947 (XB-47 prototype)

ARMAMENT 2 × 20mm Hispano cannon; 4 × .303in Browning machine guns

THE EXCEPTIONALLY FAST B-47 BOMBER HAD AN INNOVATIVE SWEPT WING AND SIX JET ENGINES HOUSED IN UNDERWING PODS

THE HUGELY POPULAR VISCOUNT WAS THE FIRST TURBOPROP AIRLINER; IT WAS QUIETER AND FASTER THAN PISTON-ENGINE PLANES

VICKERS VISCOUNT

The world's first turboprop airliner, the Vickers Viscount was one of the few British aircraft to make an impact on the American market. Hugely popular with passengers, it offered a distinctly more comfortable, quieter, and faster ride than its piston-engined equivalents, as well as giving travellers an excellent view from its relatively large windows.

The Viscount took time to find its market. The first of the breed, the Type 630, made its maiden flight in July 1948. Although almost trouble-free from the outset, its 32-passenger capacity was too low to attract airline interest.

It was only after Vickers flew the protoype of the enlarged, higher-powered 53-seat Viscount 700 in 1950 that orders flooded in, first from British European Airways and then from many other airline carriers, including several in the United States.

The 700 entered service in April 1953. In the second half of the 1950s the stretched Viscount 800 series increased passenger capacity to 69. By the 1960s turboprop airliners were going out of fashion, upstaged by the glamour of jets even on shorter routes, where they remained more efficient. Production ended in 1964, by which time 445 had been built.

"There is none of the...brazen bellow of the high-powered piston engine...Combined with a seemingly uncanny lack of vibration, this gives the impression almost of sailing through space, the engines...utterly remote from the quiet security of this cabin."

DEREK HARVEY, DESCRIBING THE VICKERS VISCOUNT

SPECIFICATION

POWERPLANT 4 x 1,990-ehp Rolls-Royce Dart RDa7/1 Mk 525 turboprop engines (Viscount Type 810)

WINGSPAN 28.6m (93ft 8½in)

WING AREA 89.5sq m (963sq ft)

LENGTH 26.2m (85ft 8in)

GROSS WEIGHT 32,886kg (72,500lb)

MAXIMUM CRUISING SPEED 576km/h at 4,572m (358mph at 15,000ft)

RANGE 2,832km with a 6,577kg (1,760 miles with a 14,500lb) payload

ACCOMMODATION 3–4 crew, up to 75 passengers, plus cabin crew

FIRST FLIGHT 16 July 1948 (Type 630 prototype)

The Douglas D-558-2 Skyrocket No. 2 research aircraft stands in front of the first production Boeing B-47A Stratojet bomber at the National Advisory Committee for Aeronautics' High Speed Research Station at Edwards Air Force Base, California, in the early 1950s.

BRISTOL BRABAZON

The Bristol Brabazon airliner was a giant of an aircraft – larger even than a Boeing 747. It was also in many ways a strikingly advanced design for its day. Yet, commercially, this huge piston-engine airliner was a total failure for the British aircraft industry.

The aircraft was named after Lord Brabazon of Tara, who headed a committee that produced a government report on British aviation that, among other things, called for construction of a large, high-speed airliner capable of crossing the Atlantic non-stop.

Work on the project began in 1943, but the sheer size of the aircraft imposed problems that took time to resolve, delaying its maiden flight until September 1949. Technologically sophisticated, the eight-engine airliner pioneered innovations such as all-powered flying controls and high-pressure hydraulics. Planned facilities included a cocktail lounge and a cinema, yet despite its vast interior, the Bristol Brabazon was intended to carry only 60–80 passengers.

Airlines doubted they could operate such a large, heavy, expensive airliner at a profit with so few passengers. Only the prototype was ever built. With no one queuing up to buy the flying Goliath, it became a political embarrassment and was ignominiously scrapped in October 1953.

"It was an expensive white elephant."

BBC REPORTER ON THE BRISTOL BRABAZON

SPECIFICATION

POWERPLANT 8 × 2,500-hp Bristol Centaurus 20 18-cylinder radial engines (geared in pairs)

WINGSPAN 70.1m (230ft)

WING AREA 494sq m (5,317sq ft)

LENGTH 54m (177ft)

GROSS WEIGHT 131,540kg (290,000lb)

MAXIMUM CRUISING SPEED 402km/h at 7,620m (250mph at 25,000ft)

RANGE 8,851km (5,500 miles)

ACCOMMODATION Crew and 72–80 passengers (Mk I); 100 passengers (Mk II)

FIRST FLIGHT 4 September 1949 (Type 167)

WHILE TECHNOLOGICALLY ADVANCED, THE HUGE BRISTOL BRABAZON WAS UNECONOMIC TO OPERATE COMMERCIALLY

THE AEROCAR COMPRISED A CAR AND A DETACHABLE ONE-PIECE STRUCTURE INCORPORATING WINGS, TAIL, AND PROPELLER

TAYLOR AEROCAR

The Aerocar was the most successful attempt yet to produce a "flying car" – a vehicle that could be both driven on the road and flown. The brainchild of US designer, Moulton B. Taylor, the Aerocar first appeared in October 1949.

It comprised a small car and a one-piece structure incorporating wings, tail section, and propeller. With wings folded, this structure could be towed behind the car.

The owner would simply drive to an airfield and there swiftly attach the wings and tail to the car, which then became the aircraft's nose and cockpit.

The car's engine was connected by a drive shaft to the propeller, mounted at the end of the tail, and the steering wheel doubled as the aeroplane's control wheel.

Perhaps surprisingly, the Aerocar proved both air- and roadworthy. It could drive at around 60mph and fly at 110mph. But like all other attempts at a "carplane", it embodied too many compromises, ending up as neither a fully satisfactory aircraft nor a desirable automobile.

In 1956 Taylor tried and failed to drum up enough orders to justify serial production of the vehicle. Only six Aerocars were built, one of which Taylor vainly converted into the improved Aerocar III in 1968. Taylor died in 1995, but at least one of his Aerocars was still flying in the early 21st century.

SPECIFICATION

POWERPLANT 1 × 150-hp Lycoming 0-320 4-cylinder horizontally opposed piston engine (Model I specification – 1954)

WINGSPAN 9.1m (30ft)

WING AREA 15.6sq m (168sq ft)

LENGTH 6.4m (21ft)

GROSS WEIGHT 953kg (2,100lb)

MAXIMUM SPEED 177km/h (110mph)

RANGE 483km (300 miles)

ACCOMMODATION 1 pilot, 1 passenger

FIRST FLIGHT 8 December 1949

"...it is far less fatiguing to fly than it is to drive a car. You don't have to watch every second for cats, dogs, children...road signs, ladies with baby carriages, and citizens who drive...against the lights."

WILLIAM T. PIPER, PRESIDENT, PIPER AIRCRAFT CORPORATION

ENGLISH ELECTRIC CANBERRA

The RAF retired its last three English Electric Canberras on 28 July 2006 after more than 55 years' service. No wonder the Canberra is regarded as one of the most successful of all Britain's military aircraft.

Designed by E.W. Petter, the Canberra was the Royal Air Force's (RAF's) first jet bomber. In concept it resembled the famous World War II Mosquito, for it was expected to survive by its speed alone and had no defensive armament. Like the Mosquito, it also had a streamlined shape, lightweight construction, and two powerful engines.

When it entered service with the RAF in 1951, the Canberra was deployed as a strategic bomber. It clocked several notable "firsts"

during the 1950s, including the first non-stop transatlantic flight by a jet and the first flight at an altitude of over 70,000ft. The Canberra served with US air forces as the Martin B-57 and was also sold to many other countries around the world.

Its combination of speed and altitude made it an excellent photo-reconnaissance platform. It was extensively used as a "spyplane", overflying the Soviet Union and various other communist states in the 1950s and 60s.

In its role as a bomber, it was used by the RAF to raid Egyptian airfields during the 1956 Suez Crisis and by the Americans and Australians during the Vietnam War.

"Flying is like sex – I've never had all I wanted but occasionally I've had all I could stand."

STEPHEN COONTS, AUTHOR, WRITING IN *THE CANNIBAL QUEEN*

SPECIFICATION

POWERPLANT 2 x 3,402kg (7,500lb) static thrust Rolls-Royce Avon Mk 109 axial-flow turbojet engines [Canberra B (I) Mk 8]

WINGSPAN 19.5m (63ft 11½in)

LENGTH 20m (65ft 6in)

GROSS WEIGHT 23,135kg (50,990lb)

MAXIMUM SPEED 902km/h (560mph)

RANGE Approx 1,399km (800 miles)

ACCOMMODATION 3 crew

FIRST FLIGHT (Prototype) 13 May 1949, (Mk 8) 23 July 1954

THE CANBERRA WAS SO FAST THAT IT WAS NOT EQUIPPED WITH DEFENSIVE WEAPONS; THIS IS A PHOTO-RECONNAISSANCE VARIANT

DE HAVILLAND COMET

The D.H.106 Comet was the world's first jet airliner, offering – for a brief and glorious moment – the fastest, most stylish passenger travel on the planet. Designed to appeal to a select clientele, it carried just 36 passengers.

The first jet passenger services, from London to Johannesburg and Colombo, were inaugurated by Comet 1s of BOAC in 1952. The heavier and longer-range Comet 1A followed, and then the Comet 2, with Rolls-Royce Avon engines.

Flying higher and faster than any other airliner, the Comet seemed assured of worldwide sales. But in 1954 two Comets inexplicably broke up while flying at high altitude off Italy. The whole fleet was grounded.

An investigation eventually found that cumulative structural fatigue had caused the metal to crack around the airliner's square windows. By the time the much-improved Comet 4 entered service with BOAC in 1958, larger and faster American jet airliners were setting a new standard in air travel. The British lead had been lost and was never regained.

SPECIFICATION

POWERPLANT 4 × 4,736kg (10,500lb) static thrust Rolls-Royce Avon Mk. 525B turbojet engines (Comet 4C)

WINGSPAN 35m (114ft 10in)

LENGTH 35.97m (118ft)

GROSS WEIGHT 73,500kg (162,000lb)

TYPICAL CRUISING SPEED 872km/h at 9,450m (542mph at 31,000ft)

RANGE 4,168km (2,590 miles) with a 8,900kg (19,630lb) payload

ACCOMMODATION 4 crew, up to 101 passengers, plus cabin crew

FIRST FLIGHT 27 July 1949 (31 October 1959 Comet 4C – G-AOVU)

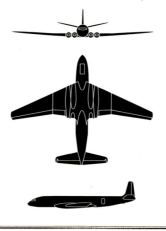

"One arrives over distant landmarks in an incredibly short time but without the sense of having travelled...One doubts one's wristwatch."

C. MARTIN SHARP, AUTHOR, ON FLYING IN THE D.H. COMET

THE COMET WAS A COMPACT, ELEGANT AEROPLANE WITH ITS FOUR TURBO-JET ENGINES SMOOTHLY BURIED IN THE WING ROOTS

THE HAWKER HUNTER'S CANNON WERE HOUSED IN THE NOSE IN A DETACHABLE PACK TO FACILITATE RE-ARMING OR MAINTENANCE

HAWKER HUNTER

Undoubtedly one of the shapeliest jet fighters, the Hawker P.1067 Hunter was a popular aircraft with pilots and crowds alike at air shows in the 1950s. Designed by Sydney Camm as a replacement for the Royal Air Force's (RAF's) Gloster Meteors, it first flew in July 1951.

It was powered by a Rolls-Royce Avon turbojet, with the air intakes in the wing roots, leaving the nose free to carry four 30mm Aden cannon. These were housed in an ingenious pack that could be easily removed and refitted for maintenance or re-arming.

The Hunter entered service as the F.1 in July 1954, but numerous early problems, including a crucial lack of range, led to its replacement a year later by the improved F.4, which could also carry rockets and bombs.

Notable among succeeding variants was the F.6, which introduced distinctive "dog tooth" wing leading edges and proved the definitive fighter version.

Although the RAF phased out its Hunter interceptors in 1963, it pressed on with the ground-attack FGA.9 until 1970, and the Royal Navy went on using FGA.11s into the late 1980s.

The Hunter also served with many foreign air forces. India employed the aircraft to good effect in its 1965 and 1971 wars with Pakistan, while Jordanian and Iraqi Hunters operated against Israeli forces in 1967 and 1973.

"I was sold on flying as soon as I had a taste for it."

JOHN GLENN, US ASTRONAUT

SPECIFICATION

POWERPLANT 1 x 4,536kg (10,000lb) static thrust Rolls-Royce Avon 203 (RA 28 rating) axial-flow turbojet engine (Hunter F.6)

WINGSPAN 11.3m (33ft 8in)

LENGTH 9.1m (45ft 10½in)

GROSS WEIGHT 11,158.56kg (24,600lb) overload weight with drop tanks

MAXIMUM SPEED 1,151km/h (715mph) at sea level

RANGE 2,961km at 829km/h (1,840 miles at 515mph) with drop tanks

ACCOMMODATION 1 crew

FIRST FLIGHT 21 July 1951 (Type 1067 – Hunter Mk 1 prototype)

SAUNDERS-ROE PRINCESS

The epitome of those large, elegant commercial flying boats that had reigned supreme on intercontinental air routes in the 1930s, the Saunders-Roe Princess had the misfortune to be born into a postwar world whose requirements had changed.

Certainly, the aircraft had ample power, with ten Bristol Proteus turboprop engines installed as coupled pairs in each of the four inboard nacelles, and as single units in the two outboard nacelles.

It also had a massive hull of "double-bubble" cross-section, which allowed space for two decks. These were to have passenger seats and refreshment bars; the lower deck also had two freight holds, while the upper deck housed the flight crew and it also had sufficient space for a galley.

However, by the 1950s landplanes had outstripped flying boats' performance, which was hampered by their drag-inducing hulls. Also, a vast wartime programme of airfield construction enabled landplanes to touch down in many of the more remote locations that were once only accessible to seaplanes.

Unfortunately, BOAC, the Princess's potential customer, had opted for an all-landplane fleet even before the flying boat made its maiden flight in August 1952. Only one prototype was ever completed. This, and two uncompleted ones, were cocooned in 1954 and scrapped in 1967.

"Both optimists and pessimists contribute to the society. The optimist invents the aeroplane, the pessimist the parachute."

GEORGE BERNARD SHAW, PLAYWRIGHT

SPECIFICATION

POWERPLANT 10 × 3,780-ehp Bristol Proteus Series 600 turboprop engines installed in six wing-mounted nacelles

WINGSPAN 66.9m (219ft 6in)

WING AREA 487.7sq m (5,250sq ft)

LENGTH 45.1m (148ft)

GROSS WEIGHT 149,688kg (330,000lb)

CRUISING SPEED 579km/h at 11,278m (360mph at 37,000ft)

RANGE 8,481km (5,270 miles)

ACCOMMODATION 6 crew, 105 passengers

FIRST FLIGHT 22 August 1952

UNABLE TO COMPETE AGAINST POSTWAR LANDPLANES, ONLY ONE PROTOTYPE OF THE ELEGANT PRINCESS WAS EVER COMPLETED

THE WORLD'S ONLY TURBOPROP BOMBER, THE TUPOLEV BEAR COMBINED PROPELLERS WITH THE SWEPT WING OF A JET AIRCRAFT

TUPOLEV Tu-95 BEAR

If the Cold War had ever turned hot, the massive Tupolev Bear is the aircraft that might have nuked New York. The Tupolev design bureau was tasked with designing an intercontinental bomber in 1951, as the Soviet Union sought a means to deliver its newly developed atomic bomb onto targets in the United States. Tupolev came up with the world's only turboprop bomber aircraft, combining propellers with the swept wing normally associated with jets.

Flown in November 1952, it entered service with the Soviet Air Force in 1957. Fast and high-flying, armed with five twin-gun turrets, it was a formidable aeroplane. Its quartet of mighty Kuznetsov turboprops, driving massive contra-rotating propellers, were powerful and fuel-efficient, although also incredibly noisy – the Bear is quite possibly the loudest aircraft ever built.

Improvements in surface-to-air and air-to-air missiles soon made it unlikely that the Bear could penetrate to a strategic target to drop a free-fall bomb, so the Tu-95K-20 model became an aerial launcher for a 400-mile-range stand-off nuclear missile, the weapon being recessed into the Bear's belly.

Like its American opposite number, the B-52, the Tupolev Bear proved adaptable to other roles and was extraordinarily durable, remaining in Russian military service in the 21st century.

"This was the crystalline moment Dan loved so well, the moment of transition between ground and air...He'd become a pilot for this very moment..."

JOHN J. NANCE, AUTHOR, WRITING IN *BLACKOUT*

SPECIFICATION

POWERPLANT 4 × 14,795-ehp Kuznetsov NK-12MV turboprop engines (Tu-95MS)

WINGSPAN 50m (164ft 2in)

WING AREA 289.9sq m (3,120sq ft)

LENGTH 49.1m (161ft 2in)

GROSS WEIGHT 187,000kg (412,257lb)

CRUISING SPEED 710km/h (441mph)

RANGE 15,000km (9,321 miles)

ACCOMMODATION 7 crew

FIRST FLIGHT 12 November 1952 (95/1 prototype)

ARMAMENT 2 × 20mm Hispano cannon; 4 × .303in Browning machine guns

The Soviet Union's massive Tupolev Tu-114 long-range turboprop airliner of the late 1950s and 1960s was developed from the Tu-95 bomber. It was the largest and fastest propeller-driven transport aircraft to enter commercial service.

WHEN THE B-52 PROTOTYPE FIRST FLEW, NO ONE IMAGINED THAT THE BOMBER WOULD STILL BE IN SERVICE IN THE 21ST CENTURY

BOEING B-52

When Boeing's B-52 Stratofortress bomber entered service with US Strategic Air Command in 1955, no one could have believed that it would still be going strong in the early 21st century.

The aircraft has undergone constant updating of equipment and extensive structural modification, but its survival in frontline service is above all a tribute to the soundness of the initial design.

Distinctive features include the extraordinarily flexible wing, prevented from dragging on the ground when taxiing by an outrigger wheel under each wingtip. The heavy weight of the four paired engine pods helps to limit wing flexing in flight.

The B-52 was built as a high-altitude intercontinental bomber capable of dropping nuclear bombs on the Soviet Union. As Soviet ground-to-air missile defences improved, the B-52 had to adapt to low-level penetration of hostile airspace, and then to carrying stand-off missiles rather than bombs. During the Vietnam War the B-52 proved itself a terrifyingly effective conventional bomber; the B-52D "Big Belly" model was capable of carrying an astonishing 60,000lb bombload.

Since the end of the Cold War the B-52H version has played a central role in US air operations in Iraq and Afghanistan. It has every chance of proving the most durable aircraft in military aviation history.

> *"Moving from the B-47 bomber to the 'Buff' [B-52] was like progressing from a sportster to a stretched limousine."*
>
> CAPTAIN GENE DEATRICK, 1950s TEST PILOT

SPECIFICATION

POWERPLANT 8 × 6,155kg (13,570lb) static thrust Pratt & Whitney J57-P-43WB turbojet engines (B-52G)

WINGSPAN 56.4m (185ft)

WING AREA 371.6sq m (4,000sq ft)

LENGTH 48m (157ft 7in), later increased to 49m (160ft 11in)

GROSS WEIGHT 221,537kg (488,000lb)

COMBAT RADIUS 6,598km (4,100 miles) with a 4,536kg (10,000lb) bombload

ACCOMMODATION 6 crew

FIRST FLIGHT 15 April 1952 (YB-52 prototype)

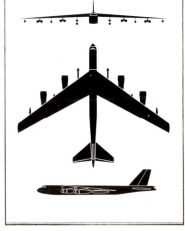

AVRO VULCAN

One of three "V bombers" designed to give Britain an "independent nuclear deterrent" in the 1950s, the Vulcan was intended to penetrate Soviet airspace at high altitude and drop free-fall nuclear bombs. In the 1960s the aircraft had to adapt to low-level attack with stand-off nuclear missiles.

The Royal Air Force's Vulcan squadrons converted to the Mk 2A version, optimized for low-level penetration missions, with more powerful Olympus engines, terrain-following radar in the nose, and passive radar warning located in a fin-top installation.

Eventually, submarine-launched Polaris missiles took over as Britain's strategic nuclear strike force, but the Vulcan made its most significant mark in history just as it was being phased out of service.

Then, in 1982, ten were rejuvenated and modified to take part in the Falklands Conflict. Flying from Ascension Island, they carried out five "Black Buck" raids against occupying Argentinian forces. These involved a 16-hour round trip of 8,000 nautical miles – the longest bombing raids in history up to that time. The last Vulcan squadron eventually disbanded on 31 December 1982.

SPECIFICATION

POWERPLANT 4 × 9,072kg (20,000lb) thrust Bristol Siddeley Olympus 301 turbojet engines (Vulcan B.Mk 2)

WINGSPAN 33.8m (111ft)

WING AREA 368.4sq m (3,965sq ft)

LENGTH 30.5m (99ft 11in)

GROSS WEIGHT 92,534kg (204,000lb)

MAXIMUM SPEED 1,038km/h (645mph)

COMBAT RADIUS 3,701km (2,300 miles)

ACCOMMODATION 5 crew

FIRST FLIGHT 31 August 1952

"Buddy of mine once told me that he'd rather fly a jet than kiss his girl. Said it gave him more of a kick."

JERRY CONNELL, *AIR CADET*, 1951

THE VULCAN WAS THE FIRST FOUR-ENGINE AIRCRAFT TO HAVE A DELTA WING

THE SUPERSONIC SUPER SABRE JET FIGHTER HAD A SWEPT WING AND AN UNDERFUSELAGE SPEED BRAKE

NORTH AMERICAN F-100 SUPER SABRE

The Super Sabre was the first US Air Force (USAF) fighter capable of supersonic speed in level flight. It marked a radical step forward in design from North American's first-generation jet fighter, the F-86 Sabre. Entering service with the USAF in November 1953, it had a 45-degree swept wing, an underfuselage speed brake, four 20mm cannon, and ranging radar in the upper lip of its oval nose air intake.

Designated the F-100 – the first of the USAF's "century series" fighters – it was definitely an exciting aircraft, but it had defects. The F-100A showed a fatal tendency to lose stability and was briefly grounded in 1955 after a series of crashes. The problem was resolved by increasing the fin area of the succeeding F-100C fighter-bomber, an aircraft which, on 20 August 1955, established the first supersonic world absolute speed record, at 822.135mph.

Next came the F-100D, the principal production version, equipped with an autopilot and adapted for in-flight refuelling. During the Vietnam War F-100s proved too heavy and insufficiently agile to make good air-to-air combat aircraft, but were used extensively for ground-attack.

The Super Sabre was the first USAF aircraft employed in the "Wild Weasel" role to detect and destroy the radar systems of enemy surface-to-air missiles.

"Flying is inherently dangerous. We like to gloss that over with…comforting statistics, but these facts remain: gravity is constant and powerful, and speed kills. In combination, they are particularly destructive."

DAN MANNINGHAM, PILOT

SPECIFICATION

POWERPLANT 1 × 7,690kg (16,950lb) thrust Pratt & Whitney J57-P-21A turbojet engine (F-100D)

WINGSPAN 11.8m (38ft 9½in)

LENGTH 15.09m (49ft 6in)

GROSS WEIGHT 15,800kg (34,832lb)

MAXIMUM CRUISING SPEED 1,435 km/h at 10,668m (892mph at 35,000ft)

RANGE 2,415km (1,500 miles) at altitude with two external fuel tanks

ACCOMMODATION 1 crew

FIRST FLIGHT 25 May 1953 – YF-100A prototype (24 January 1956 – F-100D)

BOEING 707

The Boeing 707 was the aircraft that ushered in the age of mass air travel. The first US commercial jet, it could carry many more passengers than the largest propeller-driven airliners while halving long-distance journey times. Pan Am boss Juan Trippe said of the introduction of the 707: "In one fell swoop we have shrunken the earth."

Boeing spread the cost of developing its first commercial jet by using the same prototype for a military transport. The thin swept wings with podded engines underneath were clearly derived from Boeing's jet bombers. The first production 707 flew on 20 December 1957. Pan Am rushed the aircraft into transatlantic service a month after certification, initiating a New York–London jet route on 26 October 1958. The original 707-120s were soon superseded on transoceanic services by bigger, more powerful 707-320s. The final major improvement, from 1960, was the fitting of turbofan engines to increase fuel-efficiency and range.

The 707 took the world by storm. Its smart but functional interior marked the transformation of air travel into an everyday reality, rather than an exceptional experience. In the first decade after the 707 was introduced, the volume of passengers travelling on long-distance flights worldwide quadrupled. This was truly an aircraft that changed the world.

"We're going to make the best impression on the travelling public, and we're going to make a pile of extra dough just from being first."

C.R. SMITH, AMERICAN AIRLINES, ON THE INTRODUCTION OF THE BOEING 707

SPECIFICATION

POWERPLANT 4 × 7,945kg (17,500lb) static thrust Rolls-Royce Conway Mk. 508 turbofan engines (Boeing 707-437)

WINGSPAN 43.4m (142ft 5in)

LENGTH 46.6m (152ft 11in)

GROSS WEIGHT 141,520kg (312,000lb)

MAXIMUM CRUISING SPEED 954km/h at 7,620m (593mph at 25,000ft)

RANGE 7,830km (4,865 miles) with a maximum payload of 25,855kg (57,000lb)

ACCOMMODATION 3–4 crew, up to 189 passengers, plus cabin crew

FIRST FLIGHT 15 July 1954 (Model 367-80 civil registration N70700)

THE US's FIRST COMMERCIAL JET LINER, THE BOEING 707 TURNED MASS AIR TRAVEL INTO AN EVERYDAY REALITY

TAILLESS AND WITH A DISTINCTIVE NEEDLE NOSE, THE BRITISH F.D.2 WAS CREATED TO INVESTIGATE TRANSONIC FIGHT

FAIREY F.D.2

The sleek and angular Fairey Delta 2 was the first aircraft to exceed 1,000mph in level flight. Designed by Herbert Chaplin of the Fairey Aviation Company, the F.D.2 was created to meet a British government requirement for an experimental aeroplane to investigate transonic flight – flight at or near the speed of sound.

The F.D.2 was a tailless aircraft with a needle nose. The two intakes for its Rolls-Royce Avon afterburning turbojet were in the roots of its mid-set, slender delta wing, which had 60 degrees of sweep on its leading edge.

Because the aircraft adopted a nose-high attitude on its landing approach, the pilot's view at this critical stage was significantly improved by having a nose that could be drooped by ten degrees.

The first of the two F.D.2s built flew well from the outset. Test pilot Peter Twiss took it beyond Mach 1 on 28 October 1955, reaching Mach 1.56, and then suggested an attempt on the world speed record.

On 10 March 1956 he made two measured runs in opposite directions at 38,000ft, achieving a mean speed of 1,132mph (Mach 1.73). This was an extraordinary 38 per cent faster than the previous record, set by an American Super Sabre fighter only seven months earlier. The second F.D.2 was later used for aerodynamic research in the development of Concorde.

"In the space age, man will be able to go around the world in two hours – one hour for flying and one hour to get to the airport."

NEIL McELROY, US SECRETARY OF DEFENCE, 1958

SPECIFICATION

POWERPLANT 1 × 4,763kg (10,500lb) static thrust Rolls-Royce Avon RA. 28 turbojet engine

WINGSPAN 8.2m (26ft 10in)

WING AREA 33.4sq m (360sq ft)

LENGTH 15.7m (51ft 7½in)

GROSS WEIGHT 6,078kg (13,400lb)

MAXIMUM SPEED 1,912km/h (1,188mph)

RANGE 1,336km (830 miles)

ACCOMMODATION 1 crew

FIRST FLIGHT 6 October 1954

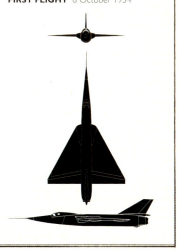

LOCKHEED F-104 STARFIGHTER

When it first appeared in 1954, the super-fast, lightweight F-104 Starfighter was dubbed "the missile with a man in it". Designed by Lockheed's Kelly Johnson, it was both small and simple – indeed, F-104s were memorably described by journalist Tom Wolfe as "chimneys with little razor-blade wings".

The first combat aircraft capable of sustaining speeds above Mach 2, the Starfighter had an outstanding rate of climb that made it, in principle, the ideal interceptor. In May 1958 it claimed both the world absolute speed and absolute height records, making it the first aeroplane ever to hold both simultaneously.

Unfortunately, the Starfighter had a poor rate of turn – a severe drawback in air-to-air combat – and could also be difficult to fly. It had some positively bad handling characteristics and unforgivingly punished pilot error.

Although the US Air Force (USAF) ordered 722 of the aircraft, it ultimately took delivery of only 296. The US's ally, West Germany, operated more F-104s than the USAF, but may have regretted it. Of 917 West German Starfighters, 270 were lost in accidents: German pilots called it "the Widowmaker".

The aircraft nonetheless flew with five NATO nations and the final production total was a highly respectable 2,580.

SPECIFICATION

POWERPLANT 1 x 7,165kg (15,800lb) static thrust General Electric J79-GE-11A afterburning turbojet engine (F-104G)

WINGSPAN 6.7m (21ft 11in)

WING AREA 18.2sq m (196sq ft)

LENGTH 16.7m (54ft 9in)

GROSS WEIGHT 13,054kg (28,779lb)

MAXIMUM SPEED 2,330km/h at 11,000m (1,450mph at 36,000ft)

COMBAT RADIUS 1,200km (745 miles) on maximum internal fuel load

ACCOMMODATION 1 crew

FIRST FLIGHT 7 February 1954 (XF-104 prototype); 5 October 1960 (F-104G)

"[Airplanes are] near perfect, all they lack is the ability to forgive."

RICHARD COLLINS, PILOT AND AVIATION WRITER

THE F-104 HAD AN OUTSTANDING RATE OF CLIMB, BUT WAS TRICKY TO FLY

THE F-4 PHANTOM IS REGARDED AS THE MOST IMPORTANT WESTERN FIGHTER OF THE 1960s

McDONNELL DOUGLAS F-4 PHANTOM II

The most significant Western fighter of the 1960s, the F-4 Phantom equipped not only the US Navy and US Air Force (USAF) but also numerous foreign air arms, including Britain's Royal Navy and Royal Air Force. It played a prominent part in the Vietnam War, proving equally effective whether operating from aircraft carriers or from land bases.

A twin-engine two-seater, the F-4 Phantom was originally designed as a shipboard interceptor to defend the US fleet against enemy intruders. The USAF subsequently adopted it as a solid and versatile fighter and ground-attack aircraft.

The Phantom was initially armed only with missiles, but the experience of air combat with North Vietnamese MiGs soon revealed the advisability of carrying a gun.

Cannon were fitted in an improvised fashion under the fuselage of many of the fighters before the USAF's definitive F-4E appeared in 1967 with a 20mm cannon beneath its nose. Although neither light nor agile enough to be an ideal air-to-air combat machine, the F-4 claimed almost 160 enemy fighters shot down in Vietnam. It also performed well in a wide range of other roles, including both reconnaissance and ground attack.

The last Phantom to see active service was the F-4G Wild Weasel version, used to knock out Iraqi radar in the 1991 Gulf War. In total, 5,195 were built.

> "*Landing on the ship during the daytime is like sex. It's either good or it's great. Landing on the ship at night is like a trip to the dentist; you may get away with no pain, but you just don't feel comfortable.*"
>
> LIEUTENANT COMMANDER THOMAS QUINN, US NAVY

SPECIFICATION

POWERPLANT 2 × 7,711kg (17,000lb) static thrust General Electric J79-GE-17 afterburning turbojet engines (F-4E)

WINGSPAN 11.7m (38ft 5in)

WING AREA 49.2sq m (530sq ft)

LENGTH 19.2m (63ft)

GROSS WEIGHT 27,502kg (60,630lb)

MAXIMUM SPEED 2,390km/h (1,485mph)

RANGE 1,690km/h (1,050 miles)

ACCOMMODATION 2 crew

FIRST FLIGHT 27 May 1958 (F4H-1); 30 June 1967 (F-4E)

MIKOYAN & GURYEVICH MiG-21

A classic dogfighter and interceptor, the MiG-21 has probably seen more combat than any other modern fighter, having taken part in at least 30 shooting wars. It was the first Soviet aircraft capable of Mach 2 in level flight, and became ubiquitous in the air forces of the Soviet Union and its allies throughout the 1960s and 70s.

Its encounters with American F-4s in Vietnam revealed a fascinating contrast of design concepts. While the United States opted for a complex, heavy two-seater packed with electronic equipment, the Soviet MiG was a stripped-down, single-seat, single-engine fighter, armed with just a couple of missiles, a cannon, and a basic radar.

However, its exceptional agility frequently allowed it to outmanoeuvre its more powerful and sophisticated opponent. It generally handled well, despite being prone to mild snaking that could cause stalls and surges in the compressor of its Tumanskii turbojet.

Cheap to produce and easy to maintain, the MiG-21 found ready markets throughout the world. The aircraft evolved over time, acquiring a more powerful engine, more advanced radar, increased fuel capacity, and more missile armament. But it remained a reliable, affordable high-performance fighter. MiG-21s served with no fewer than 56 air forces worldwide, and many were still operational in the early 21st century.

"It was superb to fly, tough, simple, and easy to build in large numbers..."

IVAN RENDALL, AUTHOR, DESCRIBING THE MiG-21 IN *ROLLING THUNDER*

SPECIFICATION

POWERPLANT 1 x 6,600kg (14,550lb) thrust Tumansky R-13F2S-300 axial-flow two-spool turbojet with modulated afterburner (MiG-21 MF)

WINGSPAN 7.2m (23ft 5½in)

WING AREA 23sq m (247½sq ft)

LENGTH (with pitot boom) 15.8m (51ft 8½in)

GROSS WEIGHT 9,661kg (21,299lb)

MAXIMUM SPEED 2,230km/h at 13,000m (1,386mph at 42,651ft)

RANGE 1,716km (1,066 miles)

THE AGILE AND SUCCESSFUL MiG-21 WAS A SIMPLE, SINGLE-ENGINE FIGHTER ARMED WITH JUST TWO MISSILES AND A CANNON

THE EXPERIMENTAL X-15 WAS BUILT TO EXPLORE THE PROBLEMS OF FLYING AT EXTREME SPEEDS AND ALTITUDES

NORTH AMERICAN X-15

The record-breaking North American X-15 was an aircraft designed specifically to push flight to its extreme limits. From June 1959 to November 1968 it made 199 experimental flights, flown by a dozen different test pilots, including future Moon-mission leader Neil Armstrong. The aim was to investigate the problems of flying at unprecedented speeds and at altitudes close to or beyond the edge of space.

Powered by a Reaction Motors single-barrel rocket motor, the X-15 had a simple basic configuration, with a tiny, unswept, tapering wing and a retractable undercarriage consisting of a nosewheel and two twin rear skids – the lower half of its ventral fin had to be jettisoned before it could land, to allow sufficient ground clearance.

Carried to around 40,000ft under the wing of a B-52 bomber, the X-15 was then released for a short but spectacular blast of rocket-driven flight. Its performance was truly incredible. The X-15 proved by far to be the fastest and highest-climbing aircraft that had ever been built.

The highest speed attained was Mach 6.72 (4,534mph), on 3 October 1967, while highest-altitude missions officially qualified as space flights. The research programme was marred by one fatal accident: on 15 November 1967 an X-15 broke up during its descent, killing test pilot Michael J. Adams.

"This is the new age of exploration; space is our great New Frontier."

JOHN F. KENNEDY, WHILE US PRESIDENTIAL CANDIDATE IN 1960

SPECIFICATION

POWERPLANT 1 x 25,855kg (57,000lb) static thrust Thiokol (Reaction Motors) XLR99-RM-2 single-chamber liquid-propellant rocket engine (NA X-15A-2)

WINGSPAN 6.7m (22ft)

GROSS WEIGHT 23,095kg (50,914lb) at launch

MAXIMUM SPEED 7,297km/h (4,534mph)

RANGE 451km (280 miles)

ACCOMMODATION 1 crew

FIRST FLIGHT 8 June 1959

The Hawker P.1127, with its unique
Bristol Pegasus engine, finally made
the vertical take-off and landing
aeroplane a practical proposition.
The outstandingly successful British
Aerospace Harrier tactical ground-
support fighter was evolved from it.

HAWKER P.1127

During the postwar period aircraft manufacturers around the world wrestled with the knotty problem of vertical take-off and landing (VTOL). The usefulness of a winged aircraft that could operate from a car park or a forest clearing was obvious, but how to design one was certainly not.

An extraordinary variety of configurations was tested – including a number of "tail-sitters" – but none proved satisfactory.

In 1957 Ralph Hooper at Hawker Aircraft began work on an aircraft to exploit "vectored thrust", an idea originally conceived by Frenchman Michel Wibault and developed by the Bristol Engine Company.

Designated P.1127, the Hawker aircraft had four rotatable nozzles that directed the efflux of its Pegasus jet engine vertically during take-off and landing, but horizontally in flight. The aircraft had a one-piece, high-set swept wing and swept conventional tail surfaces. The engine was located amidships, with fore and aft nozzles protruding on the fuselage flanks.

The first of six P.1127 prototypes made its initial tentative hover in October 1960, and by September 1961 two P.1127s were able to complete transitions from vertical to horizontal flight and vice versa.

The enigma of vertical take off and landing had finally been solved. The way was now open to development of the famous Harrier "Jump Jet", one of the most successful of modern military aircraft.

> *"…the Hawker P.1127…evolved into that typically British bit of lateral thinking, the Harrier 'Jump Jet'."*
>
> SIR RICHARD EVANS, CBE, OF BAE SYSTEMS, ON NOTABLE MILESTONES
> OF AIRCRAFT DEVELOPMENT

SPECIFICATION

POWERPLANT 1 × 5,126kg (11,300lb) Bristol Siddeley Pegasus vectored thrust turbofan engine

WINGSPAN 7.4m (24ft 4in)

LENGTH 14.9m (49ft)

GROSS WEIGHT 5,352kg (11,800lb)

CRUISING SPEED 1,160km/h (720mph)

ACCOMMODATION 1 crew

FIRST FLIGHT 21 October 1960 (tethered VTOL); 19 November 1960 (free VTOL); 7 July 1961 (conventional take-off and flight); 12 September 1961 (first double transition flight vertical to horizontal/horizontal to vertical

THE P.1127 HAD FOUR ROTATABLE NOZZLES THAT DIRECTED ITS ENGINE EFFLUX VERTICALLY DURING TAKE-OFF AND LANDING

THE FUSELAGE OF THE SUPERSONIC SR-71 WAS ACTUALLY THINNER THAN THE ENGINE PODS MOUNTED ON ITS WINGS

LOCKHEED SR-71A

One of the most amazing aeroplanes ever built, the SR-71A Blackbird originated from the CIA's request for a replacement for the U-2 spyplane. Like many top-secret projects, it was entrusted to Lockheed's famous "Skunk Works" team, headed by Kelly Johnson. They came up with the A-12 first, in 1962, and then the slightly larger SR-71, in December 1964.

The fastest air-breathing, manned aircraft, the SR-71 was designed to fly at three times the speed of sound (over 2,000mph) and at an altitude in excess of 80,000ft, overflying hostile territory on photo-reconnaissance missions. Everything about the aircraft was novel, from its heat-resistant, lightweight, titanium alloy skin to the combined turbojet/ramjet engines, super-efficient at high supersonic speed. The elongated fuselage was actually thinner than the huge engine pods mounted on the wings.

The SR-71 was finished in radar-absorbent black paint in an early attempt at "stealth". However, its survival was guaranteed not by evading radar-detection but by flying too fast and too high for a ground-launched missile to do damage.

Its cruising speed was phenomenal – it could cross the United States from coast to coast in just over an hour. The SR-71 was introduced into service in 1966; the last of these sensational aircraft retired in 1998.

SPECIFICATION

POWERPLANT 2 × 14,742kg (32,500lb) static thrust Pratt & Whitney J58-1 (JT11D-20B) continuous-bleed afterburning turbojet engines (SR-71A)

WINGSPAN 16.9m (55ft 7in)

WING AREA 167.2sq m (1,800sq ft)

LENGTH 32.7m (107ft 5in)

GROSS WEIGHT 77,112kg (170,000lb)

MAXIMUM SPEED (ABSOLUTE SPEED RECORD) Mach 3.3+ or 3,529.56 km/h (2,193.167mph)

COMBAT RANGE 5,400km (3,355 miles)

ACCOMMODATION 2 crew

FIRST FLIGHT 24 April 1962 (A-11 Oxcart); 22 December 1964 (SR-71)

"Though I fly through the Valley of Death, I shall fear no evil, for I am 80,000ft and climbing."

SIGN OVER THE ENTRANCE TO THE SR-71 OPERATING LOCATION, KADENA AIR BASE, OKINAWA

TUPOLEV Tu-22M

The sharp-featured Tu-22M was probably the most effective strategic bomber produced by the Soviet Union during the Cold War.

The Tu-22M's most distinctive feature was its variable-geometry "swing wing", popular in the 1960s as a way of reconciling the demands of supersonic flight with the need for decent performance in both take-off and landing. The bomber's engines were mounted side-by-side in the rear fuselage, and were fed air through long ducts from intakes between the cockpit and wing.

The Tu-22M did not have intercontinental range without in-flight refuelling, but its potential for mounting a supersonic, low-level attack with nuclear bombs or missiles seriously concerned the US when it entered service in the 1970s.

The Tu-22M was also deployed as an anti-shipping aircraft. It saw action as a conventional bomber during Soviet operations in Afghanistan, and in Chechenia in the 1990s. The Tu-22M remained in service in Russia and Ukraine into the 21st century.

"I have the normal desire, experienced by everybody who's ever flown an airplane with a certain amount of zoom capability, to go a little bit higher and a little bit faster."

GORDON COOPER, ASTRONAUT

THE Tu-22M's SWING WING HAD A FIXED CENTRE-SECTION TO WHICH THE PIVOTED OUTER SECTIONS WERE ATTACHED

SPECIFICATION

POWERPLANT 2 x 25,000kg (55,115lb) thrust Klimov NK-25 turbofan engines

WINGSPAN Swept 34.3m (112ft 5¾in); unswept 23.3m (76ft 5½in)

WING AREA Swept 175.8sq m (1,892½sq ft); unswept 183.6sq m (1,976¼sq ft)

LENGTH 42.5m (139ft 3¾in)

GROSS WEIGHT 124,000kg (273,369lb)

MAXIMUM SPEED 2,000km/h (1,243mph)

RANGE 7,000km (4,350 miles)

ACCOMMODATION 4 crew

FIRST FLIGHT 30 August 1964 (Tu-22M-O prototype)

NORTH AMERICAN XB-70 VALKYRIE

When it was rolled out on 11 May 1964, the first prototype of North American's XB-70 six-engine Mach 3 strategic bomber was the most expensive, most powerful, longest, and heaviest aeroplane ever built.

It had six engines housed in a box structure beneath the delta wing. In flight, the wingtips could be lowered up to 65 degrees to contain the airflow under the wing, a feature found in no other large aircraft. Flying at three times the speed of sound, the airframe temperatures were expected to exceed 330°C, so almost 70 per cent of the Valkyrie's structure was made of heat-resistant stainless steel.

The aircraft was originally intended to replace the Boeing B-52, but long before the first prototype appeared, plans to put the XB-70 into production had been cancelled. It seemed that missiles were in fashion and large, high-flying nuclear bombers were out.

The Valkyrie found a niche, however, as an experimental aircraft. After early structural problems were overcome, it performed well.

In October 1965 the second and last XB-70 maintained Mach 3.08 for 33 minutes, crossing eight US states. This aircraft was then lost in an in-flight collision with an F-104 when flying in formation for a photo-shoot on 8 June 1966. The surviving XB-70 continued research flights until February 1969.

"Flight is the only truly new sensation that men have achieved in modern history."

JAMES DICKEY, AUTHOR

SPECIFICATION

POWERPLANT 6 × 12,701kg (28,000lb) thrust General Electric YJ93-GE-3 afterburning turbojet engines

WINGSPAN 32m (105ft)

WING AREA 585sq m (6,297sq ft)

LENGTH 56.6m (185ft 10in)

WINGSPAN 9.8m (32ft 2in)

GROSS WEIGHT 249,480kg (550,000lb)

MAXIMUM SPEED Mach 3 – more than 3,220 km/h at 21,300m (2,000mph at 70,000ft)

RANGE 7,900km (4,288 miles)

FIRST FLIGHT 21 September 1964

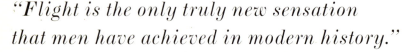

THE XB-70'S SIX POWERFUL ENGINES WERE NEATLY HOUSED IN AN UNDERWING BOX STRUCTURE.

ACCESS TO THE GALAXY'S VAST CARGO BAY IS VIA CLAMSHELL DOORS UNDER THE REAR FUSELAGE AND A HINGED NOSE VISOR

LOCKHEED C-5 GALAXY

The gargantuan Lockheed Galaxy transport aircraft is incredible for its sheer size. Ever since the four-engine C-5A was first delivered to the US Air Force's Military Airlift Command in December 1969 it has dwarfed just about every other aeroplane around.

Its vast cargo bay can accommodate two main battle tanks, six attack helicopters, or around 260,000lb of supplies. Access is through huge doors that open the aircraft from top to bottom – an upward-hinged nose visor at the front, and clamshell doors under the rear fuselage.

The General Electric TF39 turbofan, developed specifically for the Galaxy, was once the largest such engine in existence. The aircraft's "high flotation" landing gear comprises 28 wheels, allowing it to operate successfully even from unpaved airfields.

The Galaxy's range is an impressive 2,500 miles; with in-flight refuelling, it can carry on around the world until the crew collapse from exhaustion. The C-5A was notably used to ferry US military supplies to Israel during the 1973 Yom Kippur War. An improved C-5B model was introduced in the mid-1980s.

The US Air Force embarked on an ambitious modernization of its Galaxy fleet in the first decade of the 21st century, ensuring the aircraft's future as a vital contributor to US military logistics.

"When you get it right, mighty beasts float up into the sky. When you get it wrong, people die."

ROGER BACON, 13TH CENTURY ENGLISH PHILOSOPHER

SPECIFICATION

POWERPLANT 4 × 18,598kg (41,000lb) static thrust General Electric TF39-GE-1 turbofan engines

WINGSPAN 67.9m (222ft 8½in)

WING AREA 576sq m (6,200sq ft)

LENGTH 75.5m (247ft 10in)

GROSS WEIGHT 348,818kg (769,000lb)

MAXIMUM SPEED 919km/h (571mph)

RANGE 6,033km (3,749 miles)

ACCOMMODATION 6 crew

BOEING 747

When the Boeing 747 entered service in 1970 it was by far the largest, heaviest, most powerful airliner the world had ever seen. With a tail as high as a six-storey building and a wing wide enough to park more than 40 family cars on, it could carry three times as many passengers as the Boeing 707, which was then still the market leader in jet air travel.

Gambling on the success of such a massive passenger aircraft was an enormous financial risk for Boeing and its launch customer, Pan American. Many airline experts believed that the future lay with supersonic passenger jets, which would soon make the 747 obsolete. Boeing hedged its bets by designing the aircraft so that it would work equally well as a freight carrier, should passenger traffic failed to materialize.

But, as we all now know, the gamble paid off handsomely. The 747 carried forward the revolution begun by the 707, slashing seat prices to bring long-distance flight within the reach of millions. The age of mass air travel had arrived.

A further huge stride came with the introduction of the 747-400, first flown in 1988. A major redesign with upgraded engines, this variant had the range to fly popular long-haul routes, non-stop. In the first decade of the 21st century, the 747-400 remained in service with airlines worldwide.

"The Boeing 747 is the commuter train of the global village."

H. TENNEKES, AUTHOR, WRITING IN *THE SIMPLE SCIENCE OF FLIGHT*

SPECIFICATION

POWERPLANT 4 × 28,169kg (62,100lb) thrust General Electric CF6-80C2B5F turbofan engines or 4 × 28,713kg (63,300lb) thrust Pratt & Whitney PW4062 turbofan engines (Boeing 747-400ER)

WINGSPAN 64.4m (211ft 5in)

LENGTH 70.7m (231ft 10in))

GROSS WEIGHT 412,776kg (910,000lb)

CRUISING SPEED 912km/h at 10,668m (567mph at 35,000ft)

RANGE 14,205km (8,827 miles) fully loaded

ACCOMMODATION 12 flight crew, 416–524 passengers, plus cabin crew

FIRST FLIGHT 9 February 1969 (Boeing 747-100) loaded

THE BOEING 747 USHERED IN THE AGE OF THE WIDEBODY JET, BRINGING AIR TRAVEL WITHIN THE REACH OF MILLIONS

CONCORDE CRUISED EFFICIENTLY AT 1,400MPH, YET OPERATED FROM RUNWAYS DESIGNED FOR SUBSONIC AIRLINERS

CONCORDE

The world's only successful supersonic passenger carrier, Concorde was an airliner of unsurpassed elegance and a miracle of engineering. It was able to carry 128 passengers at twice the speed of sound, and once seemed to embody the future of commercial aviation.

The British and French governments agreed to build Concorde in November 1962 in the belief that airlines would inevitably want the fastest available airliner.

Concorde's performance was all that had been hoped for. Taking off from an ordinary runway, it could cruise at high altitude faster than a rifle bullet, without ruffling the comfort of it passengers.

It embodied numerous ingenious solutions to technical problems. Regardless of the aircraft's speed, variable-geometry engine air intakes kept the speed of the airflow to the engines below 300mph. A retractable visor protected the main windshield against kinetic heating at supersonic speeds. Most famously, the nose drooped to enhance the crew's view during landing, which was executed in a steep nose-up attitude.

Concorde proved expensive to maintain and run, and its passenger payload was small. Only 16 production Concordes were built, serving as luxury carriers with Air France and British Airways.

After more than 30 years in service, Concorde made its last scheduled flight on 24 October 2003.

SPECIFICATION

POWERPLANT 4 x 17,259kg (38,050lb) thrust reheat Rolls-Royce/SNECMA Olympus 593 Mk.602 turbojet engines

WINGSPAN 25.6m (83ft 10in)

WING AREA 358.3sq m (3,856sq ft)

LENGTH 61.7m (202ft 3½in)

GROSS WEIGHT 79,265kg (174,750lb)

MAXIMUM CRUISING SPEED Mach 2.05 or 2,179km/h at 15,635 km (1,354mph at 51,300 ft)

RANGE 6,380km (3,970 miles) at maximum payload at Mach 2.05

ACCOMMODATION 9 crew, 128–144 passengers, plus cabin crew

FIRST FLIGHT 2 March 1969 (001-prototype F-WTSS Toulouse, France); 9 April 1969 (002-prototype G-BSST Bristol, England)

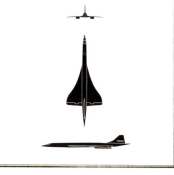

"You can be in London at 10 o'clock and in New York at 10 o'clock. I have never found another way of being in two places at once."

SIR DAVID FROST, BROADCASTER AND CONCORDE FREQUENT FLYER

Aviation has advanced tremendously since the 1970s. The advent of the widebody airliner made long-range air travel affordable to all, and aircraft operation was revolutionized by technical developments such as "glass" cockpits, fly-by-wire, and fly-by-light technologies. Refined aerodynamics improved the performance of both airliners and combat aeroplanes, while new materials such as carbonfibre made them lighter. Stealth technology dramatically altered the appearance of bombers and fighters, while weaponry continued to evolve into ever more fearsome and deadly forms. As both civil and military aircraft became more complex, development periods lengthened and cost spiralled. Meanwhile, human-powered flight became a reality, and home-built and ultralight aeroplanes proliferated as never before. Today, the triple-deck widebody airliner is a reality, the convertiplane is entering military service in the form of the Bell-Boeing Osprey, and unmanned, solar-powered aircraft with virtually unlimited endurance are waiting impatiently in the wings.

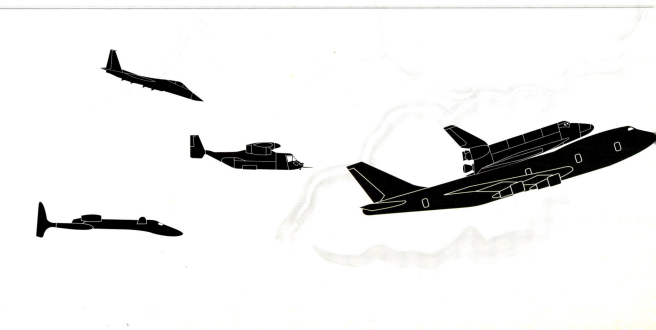

6

ANYTHING IS POSSIBLE

AIRBUS A310

Claiming the widest cabin for its length of any Airbus, the chubby A310 is essentially a truncated version of the A300. Both aircraft were built by Airbus Industrie, a government-backed European consortium formed in 1970 that posed the first real challenge to Boeing's supremacy in the jet airliner market.

Its first-born, the A300, was the first widebody certificated for a two-man cockpit crew, thus rendering obsolete the traditional flight engineer. The prototype A300B1 flew in October 1972, with two turbofan engines in its underwing pods. The larger, heavier B2 was chosen for production, entering service with Air France in May 1974. It was superseded by the B4, which carried more fuel and had more powerful engines.

The A310 entered service in 1983 and its superior range meant it was used extensively on transatlantic routes. While based on the larger A300 with the same layout, it had a redesigned wing and accommodated 280 passengers. The initial -200 series was succeeded by the extended-range -300, which made its maiden flight on 8 July 1985 and was distinguishable from the other A310 variants by its conspicuous winglets. The widespread adoption of these aircraft assured Airbus Industrie's future as a leading airliner manufacturer.

"We have clearance, Clarence. Roger, Roger. What's our vector, Victor?"

COCKPIT CREW CONVERSATION FROM THE FILM, *AIRPLANE*

SPECIFICATION

POWERPLANT 2 x 23,587kg (52,000lb) General Electric CF6-80C2 turbofans (Airbus A310-300)

WINGSPAN 43.9m (144ft)

WING AREA 219sq m (2,360sq ft)

LENGTH 46.6m (153ft 1in)

GROSS WEIGHT 164,022kg (361,600lb)

MAXIMUM SPEED 896km/h (557mph)

RANGE 9,600 km (5,965 miles)

ACCOMMODATION 2 flight crew; 220–280 passengers

FIRST FLIGHT 28 October 1972

THE A310 PROVED TO BE EXTREMELY POPULAR WITH PASSENGERS ON TRANSATLANTIC ROUTES

A PIONEER OF THE THREE-ENGINE WIDEBODY AIRLINER, THE DC-10 WAS REGARDED WITH AFFECTION BY THOSE WHO FLEW IT

McDONNELL DOUGLAS DC-10

Held in affectionate regard by pilots and engineers, the DC-10 was "fun to fly, roomy, and quiet". Yet this impressive pioneer of the three-engined, widebody airliner endured troubled beginnings. A series of accidents in the 1970s and 80s had unfortunately tarnished its reputation; however, only one of these accidents was due to a design deficiency, and this had been rectified in most DC-10 aircraft before the event in question.

The DC-10 became McDonnell Douglas's first commercial airliner following the merger between the Douglas Aircraft Company and McDonnell Aircraft Corporation in 1967. It was built to an American Airlines specification for an aircraft with the widebody appeal of the Boeing 747, capable of flying similar long-range routes from airports with shorter runways, yet smaller than the "jumbo".

With one engine beneath each wing and one located at the base of the fin, the DC-10 accommodated 250–380 passengers seated up to ten-abreast. In addition to its twin nosewheels and two four-wheel units, it also had a two-wheel central unit to spread the pavement load – a feature that won the DC-10 orders over its competitors.

The prototype flew in August 1970 and DC-10s entered service a year later. Six commercial models were built, along with one military variant.

"Flying…has changed our sense of our body, the personal space in which we live, now elastic and swift. I could be in Bombay for afternoon tea if I wished."

DIANE ACKERMAN, *NEW YORK TIMES*

SPECIFICATION

POWERPLANT typically 3 × 18,597kg (41,000lb) General Electric CF6-6D1 turbofans

WINGSPAN 47.3m (155ft 4in)

WING AREA 358.7sq m (3,861sq ft)

LENGTH 55.5m (182ft 2½in)

GROSS WEIGHT 199,580kg (440,000lb)

MAXIMUM CRUISING SPEED 940km/h (584mph)

RANGE 4,353km (2,705 miles)

ACCOMMODATION 5 flight crew, 206–380 passengers

FIRST FLIGHT 10 August 1970 machine guns

BOEING 767

The workhorse of the transatlantic route, the Boeing 767 also claims the curious merit of being the world's most slender widebody. It made its mark on commercial aviation by pioneering the now-routine Extended Twin Operating Procedures (ETOPS). ETOPS is an International Civil Aviation ruling permitting twin-engined commercial aeroplanes to fly routes that, at some points, are more than 60 minutes flying time from an emergency or diversion airport. The acronym is sometimes facetiously referred to by industry professionals as "Engine Turns or Passengers Swim".

The first of the breed, the standard 767-200, made its maiden flight in September 1981, entering service with United Air Lines the following year. It was the first large commercial aeroplane to use efficiency-enhancing "raked" wingtips. Although the 767 is built mostly of aluminium, weight-saving composites are used for many components such as control surfaces, engine cowlings, and rear wing panels.

Its unique fuselage cross-section typically seats seven abreast, and the 767's advanced two-crew flight deck has an electronic flight instrument system.

Four versions of the 767 followed, two extended-range and two stretched. Indeed, the 767 is the first widebody jetliner to be stretched twice: the 767-300 is 21ft longer than the original 767-200, and the 767-4000ER is 21ft longer than the 767-300.

SPECIFICATION

POWERPLANT (Boeing 767-300ER) typically 2 × 28,713kg (63,300lb) thrust Pratt & Whitney PW4062 turbofan engines

WINGSPAN 47.6m (156ft 1in)

WING AREA 283.3sq m (3,050sq ft)

LENGTH 54.9m (180ft 3in)

GROSS WEIGHT 186,880kg (412,000lb)

CRUISING SPEED 851km/h at 15,876m (530mph at 35,000ft)

RANGE 11,306km (7,025 miles)

ACCOMMODATION 2 flight crew, cabin crew, 218–351 passengers

FIRST FLIGHT 26 September 1981

"There is not much to say about most airplane journeys...so you define a good flight by negatives: you didn't get hijacked...you weren't late, you weren't nauseated by the food. So you're grateful."

PAUL THEROUX, AUTHOR, WRITING IN *THE OLD PATAGONIAN EXPRESS*

THE BOEING 767 WAS THE FIRST LARGE COMMERCIAL AIRLINER TO FEATURE "RAKED" WINGTIPS, WHICH INCREASE FUEL EFFICIENCY

Introduced by the Soviet Air Force in the 1980s, the supersonic Sukhoi Su-27 was part of a dazzling new generation of advanced modern fighters, capable of tackling both low-flying aircraft and cruise missiles. It has set many world records for altitude and take-off speed and, despite its size, is astonishingly agile, able to perform hard turns and hover for short periods with its nose up. Its speed and exceptional manoeuvrability have made it the star of many airshows.

BRYAN ALLEN POWERS THE GOSSAMER ALBATROSS TOWARDS THE FRENCH COAST DURING HIS RECORD-BREAKING FLIGHT IN 1979

MAcCREADY GOSSAMER ALBATROSS

The Gossamer Albatross captured headlines in 1979 when it made the first human-powered flight across the English Channel. Designed by American engineer Dr Paul MacCready, the aircraft used pedal-power to drive its large, two-bladed propeller. Appropriately, it was piloted by an amateur cyclist, Bryan Allen, who made the 22 miles and 453 yards crossing in two hours and 49 minutes, at a top speed of 19mph and an average altitude of just 5 feet.

The fragile craft resembled a giant dragonfly skimming the waves, its very long, tapering wings, spanning some 97 feet, allowing it to fly with minimal power. The craft was constructed using Mylar over a carbonfibre frame, while the wing structure incorporated expanded polystyrene ribs.

The Gossamer Albatross was MacCready's second human-powered aircraft (HPA). His first was the Gossamer Condor, winner of the first Kremer prize in 1977 for completing a specified one-mile figure-of-eight course.

MacCready then turned his attention to Kremer's £100,000 prize for a human-powered flight across the English Channel. The Gossamer Albatross first flew at Shafter, California, in July 1978. Testing and refinement continued before the aircraft was taken to England. At 5.51am on 12 June 1979 Allen took off at the foot of the cliffs near Dover and pedalled into history.

"Mon dieu, there really must be a petrol shortage in England."

BRITISH CARTOONIST SHOWING A FRENCHMAN'S REACTION TO
THE ALBATROSS'S CROSS-CHANNEL FLIGHT

SPECIFICATION

POWERPLANT 1 human
WINGSPAN 29.8m (97ft 8in)
WING AREA 43.8sq m (472sq ft)
LENGTH 10.4m (33ft 11in)
GROSS WEIGHT 31.8kg (70lb)
CRUISING SPEED 19km/h (12mph)
RANGE 35.9km (22½ miles) – achieved on flight across the English Channel
ACCOMMODATION 1
FIRST FLIGHT July 1978

FAIRCHILD REPUBLIC A-10 THUNDERBOLT II

Nicknamed the "Warthog", the A-10 Thunderbolt II was the first US Air Force jet aircraft designed for close air support of ground forces.

Certainly, it packed a mighty punch with its integrated Gatling gun. One of the most powerful aircraft cannons ever flown, it weighed as much as a Volkswagen Beetle and fired large, depleted uranium armour-piercing shells at a rate of about 3,900 rounds per minute, making short work of tanks and other ground targets.

The formidable A-10 was unleashed in response to the high number of aircraft shot down by ground air defences during the Vietnam War. An ability to withstand battle damage was vital, and the A-10 was famously capable of flying with one engine and half a wing torn off.

Moreover, the pilot was enclosed in a titanium-armour "bathtub", and the engine nacelles on either side of the rear fuselage were separated to minimize the chance of both suffering damage at the same time.

The first operational unit received "Warthogs" in 1977 and they have since proved their worth in various wars.

Production ceased in 1983, but the OA-10 Forward Air Control variant was developed to direct jets attacking ground targets. Thunderbolt IIs are still providing valuable service in Afghanistan.

SPECIFICATION

POWERPLANT 2 x 4,112kg (9,065lb) General Electric TF-34-100/A turbofans

WINGSPAN 17.5m (57ft 6in)

WING AREA 47sq m (506sq ft)

LENGTH 16.2m (53ft 4in)

GROSS WEIGHT 22,680kg (50,000lb)

MAXIMUM SPEED 676km/h (420mph)

RANGE 1,287km (800 miles)

ACCOMMODATION 1 crew

FIRST FLIGHT 10 May 1972

"Thank God for the 'Warthog', because it took some damage but it got me home."

CAPTAIN KIM CAMPBELL, US AIR FORCE, AFTER HER A-10 WAS HIT OVER BAGHDAD IN 2004

WELL-ARMOURED, THE FORMIDABLE "WARTHOG" WAS SPECIALLY DESIGNED TO PROVIDE AIR SUPPORT TO TROOPS ON THE GROUND

THE F-15 IS FANTASTICALLY FAST AND NIPPY, AND CAN CLIMB AS HIGH AS MOUNT EVEREST IN AROUND ONE MINUTE

McDONNELL DOUGLAS F-15 EAGLE

The American-built F-15 is regarded as the most formidable air-superiority fighter and interceptor in the world. Designed to replace the US Air Force's (USAF's) F-4 Phantom II, it excels in beyond-visual-range air-to-air missions and attack. Highly manoeuvrable and super-fast (up to Mach 2.5), it can deploy from the United States as far as Europe without refueling.

The F-15 has advanced aerodynamics and uses titanium extensively in its airframe. This, combined with its powerful Pratt & Whitney engines, enables it to sustain high speeds at high altitudes – it can climb an incredible 30,000ft in around 60 seconds.

Sophisticated weapons systems guide its eight missiles and aim its internal 20mm Vulcan rotary cannon.

Deliveries of the F-15A started in November 1974; six single- and twin-seat variants followed, which were used by various air forces around the world, including Israel, Japan, and Saudi Arabia. During a memorable Israeli Air Force training dogfight in 1983, an F-15D variant proved it could still land after the spectacular loss of one wing. And in 1985 an F-15A was dispatched by the USAF to destroy an orbiting satellite, leading its pilot, Major General Doug Pearson, to say, "Even space is no longer a safe zone from the mighty Eagle."

SPECIFICATION

POWERPLANT 2 x 10,855kg (23,930lb) Pratt & Whitney F-100-229 turbofans (F-15C)

WINGSPAN 13m (42ft 9in)

WING AREA 56.5sq m (608sq ft)

LENGTH 19.4m (63ft 9in)

GROSS WEIGHT 30,845kg (68,000lb)

MAXIMUM SPEED mach 2.5 or 2,660km/h (1,653mph)

RANGE 5,552km (3,450 miles)

ACCOMMODATION 1–2 crew

FIRST FLIGHT 27 July 1972

"Even as I speak, F-15s are flying over our major cities and along our borders protecting our nation. [They are going] overseas, speaking to our enemies in what seems to be the only language they understand."

LIEUTENANT COLONEL TROY FONTAINE, USAF, ON THE F-15's 30TH ANNIVERSARY IN 2002

LOCKHEED MARTIN F-16 FIGHTING FALCON

Originally developed by General Dynamics, the F-16 became one of the most important fighters of the 20th century. It was the first fighter to use "fly-by-wire" technology, whereby the flight controls are operated via electric signaling through a sidestick in the cockpit. This led to pilots saying, "You don't fly an F-16, it flies you."

Smaller and cheaper than the F-15, the F-16 it is an extremely manoeuvrable and versatile aircraft. As a result, it is a superb dogfighter, and its large, clear canopy gives the pilot an outstanding all-round view. The excellent F-16 also has a ground-attack capability. Nicknamed the "Viper", it has a mid-wing design with a blended wing/body and a cropped delta wing.

The prototype first flew in February 1974, but the F-16A and F-16B trainer production aircraft, delivered from 1979, were larger with greater fuel capacity. As well as serving with the US Air Force, the F-16 was acquired by many other nations, including NATO allies.

Continuous upgrades and improvements to the aircraft's engine, systems, and equipment produced numerous variants, including the specialist F-16 air defence fighter for the US Air Force, armed with the AIM-7 missile. F-16s have participated in numerous conflicts, most of them in the Middle East.

"Normally one can't judge a book by its cover – but the Viper is an awesome machine wrapped up in a sleek, stylish, package."

CAPTAIN LOUIS A. DAVENPORT, US AIR FORCE

SPECIFICATION

POWERPLANT 1 × 10,782kg (23,770lb) Pratt & Whitney F100-PW-220 turbofan

WINGSPAN 9.9m (32ft 8in)

WING AREA 27.9sq m (300sq ft)

LENGTH 15m (49ft 5in)

GROSS WEIGHT 19,187kg (42,300lb)

MAXIMUM SPEED 2,172km/h, or Mach 2.05 at 12,191km (1,350mph at 40,000ft)

RANGE 3,200km (2,000 miles) ferry range

ACCOMMODATION 1 crew

FIRST FLIGHT 2 February 1974 cannon; 4 × .303in Browning machine guns

ONE OF THE MOST OUTSTANDING FIGHTERS OF THE 20TH CENTURY, THE FAST-STRIKING F-16 WAS NICKNAMED THE "VIPER"

SURPRISINGLY AGILE FOR ITS SIZE, THE SUKHOI Su-27 IS A FORMIDABLE LONG-RANGE AIR-SUPERIORITY FIGHTER

SUKHOI Su-27

An old hand at dazzling air show spectators all over the world, the supersonic Sukhoi Su-27 is astonishingly agile for its size. However, this potent long-range air-superiority fighter presented serious problems during tests in its original form as the T10. Seven prototypes and a complete redesign later, it emerged with a brand new wing, undercarriage, and fuselage, as well as a large air brake on its spine.

It entered production in 1985 as the new jewel of the Soviet Air Force, more than able to match its plucky American rival, the F-15 Eagle. Built in large numbers for the Soviet Air Force, it was a significant advance over previous generations of Soviet fighters.

The Su-27's advanced avionics make it a formidable opponent, able to tackle low-flying aircraft and cruise missiles. It has a 30mm cannon in its starboard wing root, and can carry up to ten air-to-air missiles.

The Su-27PD variant was a dedicated aerobatic-display aircraft, while the Su-27SK and Su-27SMK are export versions. Some 550 Su-27s were built.

Many remain in service with Russia and various other powers, including China, Syria, and Vietnam.

"Know and use all the capabilities in your airplane. If you don't, sooner or later, some guy who does use them all will kick your ass."

DAVE "PREACHER" PACE, US NAVY

SPECIFICATION

POWERPLANT 2 × 12,519kg (27,600lb) thrust Lyulka AL-31F turbofans

WINGSPAN 14.7m (48ft 3in)

WING AREA 62sq m (667sq ft)

LENGTH 21.9m (71ft 10in)

GROSS WEIGHT 33,000kg (72,751lb)

CRUISING SPEED 2,150km/h (1,336mph)

RANGE 3,900km (2,423 miles) ferry range

ACCOMMODATION 1 crew

FIRST FLIGHT 20 May 1977

LOCKHEED F-117A NIGHTHAWK

With its menacing demeanour and black, futuristic design, the distinctive F-117A Nighthawk was the first operational aircraft entirely designed around stealth technology. Dubbed the "Bat Plane", its extraordinary appearance results from the use of "faceting" – critically angled flat surfaces – to minimize its radar signature; it is also almost entirely covered by matt black radar-absorbent material.

Interestingly, the Nighthawk gains its lift from numerous whirling vortices created by these faceted surfaces; also, the blending of the flat wing undersurfaces into the fuselage turns the whole underside into a lifting surface. Its unique design provides exceptional combat capabilities and it is equipped with sophisticated navigation and attack systems – the pilot can fly without ever having to look up from the multi-function display screens in front of him.

The Nighthawk has the advantage of being air-refuelable and, despite its size and power, it is also extremely agile.

A direct decendant of Lockheed's 1975 *Have Blue* stealth prototype programme, the Nighthawk's two prototypes were difficult to fly, but proved the idea sound. In 1982 the first of 59 F-117 fighter/attack aircraft was delivered to the US Air Force. Unveiled to the public in 1988, the Nighthawk played a major role in *Desert Storm*, the 1991 war with Iraq.

"Fight to fly, fly to fight, fight to win."

US NAVY FIGHTER WEAPONS SCHOOL, TOPGUN

SPECIFICATION

POWERPLANT 2 x 4,808kg (10,600lb) General Electric F404-F1D2 turbofans

WINGSPAN 13.2m (43ft 4in)

WING AREA 72.5sq m (780sq ft)

LENGTH 19.4m (63ft 9in)

GROSS WEIGHT 23,814kg (52,500lb)

MAXIMUM SPEED 1,127km/h (700mph)

RANGE 861km (535 miles)

ACCOMMODATION 1 crew

FIRST FLIGHT 18 June 1981

CURRENTLY USED FOR NIGHT-TIME MISSIONS ONLY, THE USAF IS NOW EVALUATING THE F-117A NIGHTHAWK FOR DAYLIGHT OPERATIONS

ROCKWELL INTERNATIONAL SPACE SHUTTLE

Punching skywards, the Space Shuttle is launched vertically like a rocket; it operates as a spacecraft, yet returns to Earth as a glider. The first orbital spacecraft designed for partial reuse, it comprises the Orbital Vehicle and two Solid Rocket Boosters, both reusable, and an expendable External Tank. Only the orbiter, resembling an aircraft with double delta wings, goes into orbit; its tank and boosters are jettisoned during ascent.

On re-entering Earth's atmosphere at 300,000ft, elevons mounted at the trailing edge of the wings take over to control roll and pitch. The craft crosses the Californian coast at 100,000ft and Mach 5 but reduces speed rapidly; when line-up begins for the runway, its speed slows to Mach 2.5 at 82,000ft. Full aerodynamic control is gained as the thrusters are deactivated: the Shuttle is now an inefficient glider and must be landed first time, every time.

Once likened to a "space truck", the Shuttle has proved a versatile craft, ferrying large payloads to various orbits, providing crew rotation for the International Space Station, and performing servicing missions. The five shuttles have flown more than 116 missions; two of these – *Columbia* and *Challenger* – were tragically lost.

SPECIFICATION

POWERPLANT 3 x 178,624kg (393,800lb) thrust Rocketdyne rocket engines

WINGSPAN 23.8m (78ft 1in)

WING AREA 249.9sq m (2,690sq ft)

LENGTH 37.2m (122ft 2in)

GROSS WEIGHT 108,864kg (240,000lb)

MAXIMUM SPEED 27,875km/h (17,321mph)

CROSSRANGE 2,009.4km (1,248½ miles)

ACCOMMODATION 7 crew

FIRST FLIGHT 12 April 1981 (Columbia OV-102)

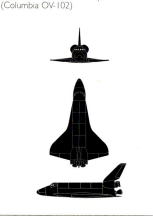

"This vehicle is performing like a champ. I've got a super spaceship under me."

BOB CRIPPEN, SPACE SHUTTLE COLUMBIA PILOT AFTER FIRST FLIGHT

THE ORBITER VEHICLE RETURNS TO EARTH AS AN ENORMOUS GLIDER

During the final stages of its return
to Earth from orbit, NASA's Space
Shuttle becomes the world's fastest,
heaviest, and most inefficient glider.
It is launched vertically like an
ordinary rocket.

RUTAN VOYAGER

The first aircraft to fly non-stop around the world without refuelling, Voyager completed its epic flight on 23 December 1986. The gruelling round trip from Edwards Air Force Base in California, took nine days, three minutes, and 44 seconds.

Voyager was designed by engineer Burt Rutan and piloted by his brother, Dick, together with Jeana Yeager. It began as little more than a sketched idea on a napkin during a lunch in 1981. To realize their dream of non-stop circumnavigation, the Rutans needed an aircraft that was light enough to reach maximum efficiency, strong enough to sustain extremely long distance flight, and capable of carrying enough fuel for the entire journey. Voyager was the result.

Made almost entirely of lightweight space-age composites, Voyager's design was geared towards maximum fuel efficiency. Although both of the light, fuel-efficient petrol engines were used during take-off and landing, only the aft engine was used in flight. The pilots were housed in a slender central nacelle split into a telephone-box-sized cockpit and a cramped cabin. Rutan's trademark canard, an extra wing at the front of the fuselage, helped maximize speed; to increase rigidity, both canard and main wing were attached to the fuselage and outriggers.

"I'm doing essentially the same kind of thing I did when I was as a kid except I'm doing it with rocket ships and airplanes and special vehicles."

BURT RUTAN, VOYAGER'S DESIGNER

SPECIFICATION

POWERPLANT 1 × 130-hp Teledyne Continental O-240 piston engine (forward) 1 × 110-hp Teledyne Continental IOL-200 piston engine (aft)

WINGSPAN 33.7m (110ft 8in)

WING AREA 33.7sq m (362sq ft)

LENGTH 8.9m (29ft 2in)

GROSS WEIGHT in excess of 4,400kg (9,700lb)

CRUISING SPEED 186km/h (116mph)

RANGE 40,210km (24,986 miles)

FIRST FLIGHT 22 June 1984

VOYAGER'S 17 FUEL TANKS CARRIED 7,011LB OF FUEL – MORE THAN 72 PER CENT OF ITS GROSS WEIGHT AT TAKE-OFF

THE DIMENSIONS OF THE An-225 ARE STAGGERING; IT IS ALMOST AS BIG AS A FOOTBALL PITCH

ANTONOV An-225

Designed to carry a Buran spacecraft externally in a somewhat bizarre "piggy-back" arrangement, the Antonov An-225 Mriya was the heaviest and most powerful aircraft ever built.

So large that it dwarfed even a Boeing 747, it was essentially a stretched version of the An-124, which was a four-engine, heavylift military and civil transport aircraft.

With the addition of twin fins, the An-124 might have proved capable of carrying the spacecraft. However, engineers realized that by inserting a massive new wing centre-section with two more engines and stretching the existing fuselage, they could create a much more versatile aeroplane.

To distribute its vast weight when fully loaded, the six-engined aircraft was equipped with an increased-capacity landing gear system with 32 wheels. Twenty of these were steerable, making the An-225 exceptionally manoeuvrable. A modified split tail also maintained the plane's airborne manoeuvrability when carrying large exterior loads. The 141ft cargo hold was designed to accommodate 80 family-size cars.

The An-225 first flew on 21 December 1988. Flights carrying the Buran spacecraft began in May 1989, but when the Russian space programme collapsed the massive plane was mothballed. In the late 1990s the An-225 was re-engined and modified, and made commercially available for transporting ultra-heavy freight.

> *"Man must rise above the Earth – to the top of the atmosphere and beyond – for only thus will he fully understand the world in which he lives."*
>
> SOCRATES, GREEK PHILOSOPHER

SPECIFICATION

POWERPLANT 6 × 23,406kg (51,600lb) thrust ZMKB Progress D-18 turbofans

WINGSPAN 88.4m (290ft)

WING AREA 905sq m (9,741½sq ft)

LENGTH 84m (275ft 7in)

GROSS WEIGHT 640,000kg (1,410,935lb)

CRUISING SPEED 750km/h (466mph)

RANGE 4,000 km (2,486 miles)

ACCOMMODATION 6 crew, 70 passengers/payload up to 250,000kg (551,146lb)

FIRST FLIGHT 21 December 1988 cannon; 4 × .303in Browning machine guns

BELL-BOEING V-22 OSPREY

The V-22 Osprey is the first aircraft specifically designed to meet the needs of all four US armed services. Cleverly combining the attributes of both helicopter and aeroplane, the aircraft takes off and lands like a helicopter using its tilting "proprotors" but, once airborne, its engine nacelles can be rotated to convert it to a turboprop airplane. Twice as fast as a helicopter with a much longer range, it has multi-mission capability ranging from combat support to medevac.

Developed as a joint project by Bell Helicopter Textron and Boeing's Helicopters Division, the V-22 is based on the XV-15 tilt-wing aircraft tested by Bell in the late 1970s.

It has a conventional fuselage, largely built from composites, with a ventral loading ramp at the rear. Mounted on top of the fuselage, the wing has a complex flap/aileron system, and swivelling pods at the wingtips house the two Allison turbines driving 38ft-diameter "proprotors". All critical systems are triple-redundant, some being armoured or designed to withstand ballistic impact.

Due to its radical design, the V-22 programme has been plagued by controversy, various technical difficulties, spiralling costs, and even cancellation threats. The Osprey is currently scheduled to enter front-line service in Iraq with the US Marines in 2007.

"The Osprey will provide our Marines with a needed edge in the complex operations they will face while defending...American interests in the 21st century."

GENERAL JAMES L. JONES, US MARINES CORPS

SPECIFICATION

POWERPLANT 2 x 6,150-hp Rolls-Royce/Allison T406-AD-400 turboshafts

WINGSPAN WITH PROPROTORS FULLY HORIZONTAL 25.5m (83ft 9½in)

BLADE AREA 24.3sq m (261.52sq ft)

LENGTH 5.5m (57ft 4in)

GROSS WEIGHT 27,443kg (60,500lb)

CRUISING SPEED 396km/h (246mph) at sea level

RANGE 4,476km (2,781 miles) ferry range

ACCOMMODATION 2 crew, 24 fully-equipped troops or 12 litters

FIRST FLIGHT 19 March 1989

THE INNOVATIVE V-22 OSPREY NIFTILY FOLDS INTO A COMPACT SIZE FOR SHIPBOARD STOWAGE

NORTHROP GRUMMAN B-2A SPIRIT

The formidable B-2 Spirit is an American multi-role stealth bomber capable of not only penetrating sophisticated enemy defences, but also of attacking heavily defended targets with both nuclear and conventional weapons.

Aware that Northrop's flying-wing bombers of the late 1940s had been difficult to track on radar, the US Air Force approached the company in the 1970s when it required a subsonic bomber to penetrate Soviet airspace undetected. The resulting B-2, using fly-by-wire to overcome instability and "low-observable" design techniques to render it "stealthy", first flew in July 1989.

The radical blending of low-observable technologies with high aerodynamic efficiency and large payload gives the B-2 important advantages over previous bombers.

Virtually an all-wing aeroplane, with its crew and 40,000lb bomb load housed in the bulbous centre section, the B-2 has four turbofan engines installed in pairs on either side. Their intakes and orifices are located above the wing where they are shielded against detection.

The first operational B-2A was delivered in December 1993, and B-2As made their debut in Kosovo in 1999. Since then, they have operated over Afghanistan and in Iraq.

SPECIFICATION

POWERPLANT 4 x 7,847kg (17,300lb) General Electric F118-GE-100 turbofans

WINGSPAN 52.4m (172ft)

WING AREA 464.5sq m (5,000sq ft)

LENGTH 21m (69ft)

GROSS WEIGHT 170,554kg (376,000lb)

MAXIMUM SPEED 764km/h (475mph)

RANGE 11,110km (6,900 miles)

ACCOMMODATION 2 crew

FIRST FLIGHT 17 July 1989

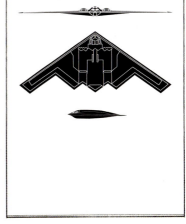

"There are only two types of aircraft – fighters and targets."

DOYLE "WAHOO" NICHOLSON, US MARINE CORPS

THE B-2A IS THE MOST EXPENSIVE PLANE EVER BUILT – EACH ONE COST UP TO $2.2 BILLION

PROTEUS HAS AN UNUSUAL TANDEM-WING AND TWIN-BOOM DESIGN WITH REAR-MOUNTED TURBOFAN ENGINES

SCALED COMPOSITES PROTEUS

Cruising higher than supersonic transports can fly, the Proteus is a unique aircraft designed for high-altitude telecommunications or science missions of long duration. Created by Burt Rutan and built by Scaled Composites, it has an unconventional tandem-wing and twin-boom design with two rear-mounted turbofan engines.

Proteus has an all-composite airframe and its span can be increased to an impressive 92 feet by adding wingtip extensions. Normally flown by two pilots in a pressurized cabin, it can also fly semi-autonomously or be flown remotely from the ground.

Rutan envisions the Proteus as a revolutionary high-altitude platform for telecommunications, reconnaissance, and commercial imaging – work now done by satellite. Other proposed roles include a space launch platform for unmanned missions.

Proteus can perform multiple missions, carrying various payloads on a ventral pylon to altitudes above 60,000 feet, remaining on station for up to 14 hours.

Flight-testing began in July 1998 and it appeared at the 1999 Paris Air Show, having flown there non-stop from Maine, in the United States. The aircraft has been used for several significant research projects and missions, including a NASA programme to measure ocean characteristics and testing of the airborne laser system.

Now owned by Northrop Grumman, Proteus is being marketed as a research platform.

"It's like a big old Cadillac. It's very quiet. The engine is way in the back."

MICHAEL MELVILL OF SCALED COMPOSITES, ON THE PROTEUS

SPECIFICATION

POWERPLANT 2 × 1,043kg (2,300lb) Williams International FJ44-2 turbofans

WINGSPAN 23.6m (77ft 6in)

WING AREA (INCLUDING CANARDS) 44.5sq m (479¼ sq ft)

LENGTH 17.2m (56ft 4in)

GROSS WEIGHT 5,670kg (12,500lb)

MAXIMUM SPEED 507km/h (315mph)

RANGE 772km (480 miles)

ACCOMMODATION 2 crew

FIRST FLIGHT 26 July 1998

NASA DRYDEN HELIOS

The forerunner of 21st-century solar-powered "atmospheric satellites", the extraordinary Helios was a remotely piloted flying wing designed for sustained flight at the very edge of space. It was developed by AeroVironment and NASA's Dryden Research Center to demonstrate sustained flight at almost 100,000 feet, and non-stop flight for at least 24 hours – 14 of which had to be above 50,000 feet.

Five underwing pods, one at each joint, carry a two-wheel undercarriage, the battery power system, flight control computers, and data instrumentation. For initial flight tests in 1999, the 14 electric motors were powered by lithium battery packs. However, in 2000 this role was taken over by solar panels on the wing's upper surface.

Helios's only flight controls were 72 elevators for pitch control; turning was accomplished by varying the power of the motors. Take-off and landing speeds were sedate, similar to the average speed of a bicycle. Coincidentally, its two rear wheels were those of a mountain bicycle; it had two smaller "scooter" wheels on the front.

Helios set a world record for sustained horizontal flight by a winged aircraft, reaching 96,863 feet on 13 August 2001. In the future, such aircraft could be used to fly autonomously for up to six months at a time on science and commercial missions.

"[This is a step towards...] flying an eternal airplane that could be sent on missions spanning months."

JOHN DEL FRATE OF DRYDEN, ON THE FUTURE FOR HELIOS

SPECIFICATION

POWERPLANT 14 × 2-hp motors

WINGSPAN 75.3m (247ft)

WING AREA 183.6sq m (1,976sq ft)

LENGTH 3.7m (12ft)

GROSS WEIGHT Up to 929kg (2,048lb)

CRUISING SPEED 31–43km/h (19–27mph) at low altitude and 274km/h (170 mph) at high altitude

ENDURANCE Theoretically unlimited – depending on power source (but see above)

ACCOMMODATION Pilot-less vehicle

FIRST FLIGHT On or about 8 September 1999

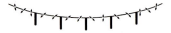

THE CURIOUS-LOOKING FLYING WING, HELIOS, WAS BUILT PRIMARILY OF COMPOSITE MATERIALS AND ASSEMBLED IN SIX SECTIONS

On 4 October 2004 Scaled Composites' SpaceShipOne, released from its White Knight carrier aircraft at 47,100ft and piloted by Brian Binnie, became the first manned spacecraft to exceed an altitude of 328,000ft twice within a 14-day period, thus winning the $10 million Ansari Prize. A fleet of commercial sub-orbital SpaceShipTwos and White Knight Two launch aircraft is now planned.

GLOBALFLYER'S SINGLE WILLIAM'S FJ44-3 JET ENGINE IS SET ABOVE THE TINY, CENTRALLY-LOCATED, PRESSURIZED COCKPIT

VIRGIN ATLANTIC GLOBALFLYER

Piloted by adventurer Steve Fossett, GlobalFlyer flew into the record books on 3 March 2005 having achieved the first solo, non-stop, jet-powered, and unrefuelled flight around the world. It was designed specifically for the purpose by Burt Rutan of Scaled Composites and part-sponsored by Virgin Atlantic.

GlobalFlyer is made entirely of composite materials and is extremely lightweight. Described as a "fuel tank with room for one", the unconventional slender-winged monoplane has two enormous fuel-filled booms on either side of the main fuselage. Fossett had to remain constantly alert throughout his round-the-world journey in order to redistribute the fuel and maintain the aircraft's balance. The flight also had its hair-raising moments: the satellite navigation system failed temporarily, and there was a mysterious fuel loss early in the flight.

Fossett left Salina, Kansas, on 1 March 2005 and returned 67 hours and 2 minutes later on 3 March, having covered a distance of some 22,870 miles.

The following year, on 8 February 2006, Fossett set a new world record in GlobalFlyer for the longest distance flown non-stop. He took off from NASA's Kennedy Space Center in Florida and landed at Bournemouth, England, on the 11th, having covered 26,389 miles in 76 hours and 45 minutes.

"I feel great. Well, yes, I could do with a shower and I could do with a little sleep, but I really do feel great."

STEVE FOSSETT, ON COMPLETING HIS HISTORIC ROUND-THE-WORLD
FLIGHT IN GLOBALFLYER

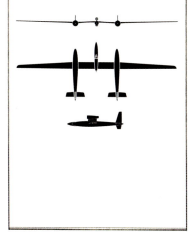

SPECIFICATION

POWERPLANT 1 x 1,043kg (2,300lb) Williams International FJ44-3 ATW turbofan

WINGSPAN 34.8m (114ft)

WING AREA 37.2sq m (400sq ft)

LENGTH 13.4m (44ft 1in)

GROSS WEIGHT 9,979kg (22,000lb)

MAXIMUM SPEED 459km/h (285mph)

RANGE Still air 33,795km (21,000 miles)

ACCOMMODATION 1 pilot

FIRST FLIGHT 5 March 2004

AIRBUS A380

Claiming to be the most spacious and advanced airliner ever built, the Airbus A380 is the world's first triple-decked "superjumbo" jet.

The only true competitor to the Boeing 747, it has been developed in response to growing airport congestion and overburdened air traffic control systems.

There are two models, the A380-800 seating up to 555 passengers, and the -800F freighter. The cockpit is set between the upper and main decks, and its layout, procedures, and handling characteristics are similar to those of other Airbus aircraft. Typically, passengers will be seated on the two upper decks with freight on the lower; however, some cargo compartments could become shops, lounges, or even casinos.

The A380 will have wider seats and aisles as well as 10–15 per cent more range, lower fuel burn and emissions, and less noise. Although taxiways may need widening, the A380 is compatible with existing runways at most major airports, and its 22-wheel undercarriage ensures that its vast load is spread.

The first A380-800 made its maiden flight in April 2005, but its delivery programme has suffered delays. Service entry, with Singapore Airlines, is due in 2007. Five aircraft are taking part in the test programme.

SPECIFICATION

POWERPLANT 4 × 38,10kg (84,000lb) Rolls-Royce Trent 900 turbofans

WINGSPAN 79.8m (261ft 10in)

WING AREA 845sq m (9,096sq ft)

LENGTH 72.75m (238ft 8in)

GROSS WEIGHT 560,000kg (1,234,568lb)

CRUISING SPEED 903km/h (561mph)

ACCOMMODATION 2 flight crew, 555–853 passengers

FIRST FLIGHT 27 April 2005

"...perfect. You can handle this large aircraft as you can handle a bicycle."

JACQUES ROSAY, A380 TEST PILOT

THE TRIPLE-DECKED A380, WHICH MAY EVEN HAVE SHOPS AND LOUNGES ON BOARD, PROMISES TO BE THE MOST SPACIOUS AIRLINER EVER

INDEX

ACKNOWLEDGMENTS

PUBLISHER'S ACKNOWLEDGMENTS

Dorling Kindersley would like to thank Angela Wilkes for editorial support, Anna Plucinksa for help with design, Adam Walker and Vania Cunha for DTP and production assistance, Raewyn Stenhouse for image scanning, Caroline Hunt for proofreading, and Dorothy Frame for compiling the index. Thanks also to Geoff Nutkins at the Shoreham Aircraft Museum for assistance in contacting Captain Eric Brown.

PHILIP JARRETT was assistant editor of *Aeroplane Monthly* magazine from its launch in 1973 until 1980, before serving ten years as production editor of Flight International magazine. Now a freelance writer and editor, he has produced countless articles and papers on a wide variety of aeronautical subjects, as well as lecturing both in England and abroad. He is the author/series editor of a number of books on various aspects of aviation history.

CAPTAIN ERIC "WINKLE" BROWN CBE, DSC, AFC is regarded as a living legend among the world's test-pilot fraternity. This highly decorated former Royal Navy officer and renowned test pilot has made an outstanding contribution to aviation, especially to the development of British naval aviation, and he has flown more aircraft types than anyone else in history.

PICTURE CREDITS

The publisher would like to thank the following for their kind permission to reproduce their photographs:

© Airbus SAS 2006 356/357
AirTeamImages/© Chris Sheldon 312,/© Steve Morris 321,/© Paul Dopson 345
Aviation-Images.com 322, 334
Captain Eric Brown 4;
Cody Images 134
© John Dibbs/Aviation-Images.com 327
The Flight Collection 298/99, 332, 342
Mark Greenberg/mgvisions.com 341, 352/53
NASA 336, 337
NASA-HQ-GRIN 338, 339
NASA Dryden Flight Research Center Photo Collection. Photo by Patrick Wright 348; Photo by Nick Galante/PMRF 351
© Sergey Sergeyev/Aviation-Images.com 323
© VirginAtlanticGlobalFlyer 354
© Mark Wagner/Aviation-Images.com 304/305

All artwork silhouettes © DK
All other images © Philip Jarrett